LINGUISTICS IN THE ELEMENTARY SCHOOL

GERTRUDE A. BOYD
ARIZONA STATE UNIVERSITY

F. E. PEACOCK PUBLISHERS, INC. ITASCA, ILLINOIS 60143

Contents

PART THREE: EMPHASES IN THE NEW GRAMMAR

Foreword to Language Arts Series

THE LANGUAGE ARTS are the core of the elementary school program. They are a vital and central force in the living and learning of young people—providing the foundation for practically all classroom activities and serving to interrelate the many areas of the curriculum. Thus, quality teaching of the language arts is essential to the entire program of the school as well as crucial to each child's learning.

Most of the language arts textbooks used in teacher education treat the total spectrum of the language arts, and few supplementary materials are available. So this series of paperback books came to be because of the editor's conviction that certain topics of the elementary school language arts need to be explored in thoroughness and depth by authors with a particular competence and interest in the topics.

In writing the books, the authors have made every attempt to be practical and specific—yet open-ended. In this way, the series is appropriate for undergraduate elementary education students and the elementary school classroom teachers who want to design and implement an effective program of language arts for children. The books could also be used to good advantage by consultants and participants in workshops and other professional renewal projects for elementary school teachers.

Paul C. Burns, Editor
The University of Tennessee

Preface

INTEREST IN LINGUISTICS among elementary school teachers has fluctuated between casual and intense. For some years the subject has been in the air at professional meetings—sometimes earnestly advocated, sometimes bitterly combatted, often provoking questions which have raised further questions rather than suggesting answers teachers could apply to their classroom procedures. Available textbooks have restrained rather than promoted the implementation of linguistic principles in the teaching of grammar, usage, and semantics.

There is great need for materials which will interpret some of the vast amount of linguistic literature into forms usable by the teacher. There is also need for acquaintanceship with intensive research in the field, with the changing emphasis in the curriculum, and with textbooks giving information on the English language, especially general usage of American English.

The book is divided into three parts, each quite different in nature.

Some readers could consider all the material essential in extending their knowledge of our language; others with a background in linguistics may consider some sections of only marginal interest.

Part One establishes the historical background for the language we use today. Since language has a character of its own which has been developed by the generations who have used it, knowing a language well helps one to know the peoples who have made it and are now making it. Americans have adapted the English language to their purposes, and American English has added vigor and color in a distinctive manner. As Americans we have accepted the English language but have changed pronunciations and meanings; we have added many words and phrases peculiar to the American way of life. English grammars, however, have histories and their current positions are the consequence of their pasts. This section establishes the principle that languages, which include American English, are subject to constant growth and decay.

In Part Two the language acquisition of the young child is discussed. This language basis is expanded by the school-age child and by the adult. The growth of language in the young child is shown through research studies which trace the development of speech from the first sounds through the use of sentences. Thus the teacher is helped to gain an understanding of the imitative speech of the young child in the early stages and his later ability to construct his own phrases and sentences which explain his meaning to others.

One of the new emphases in grammar explored in Part Three is the varied use of words and meanings over the years. The continued addition of new words, word forms, and meanings makes our language ever changing. This is evident in the different interpretations of the sentence or utterance as a unit. Increased knowledge about semantics adds to understanding of words, meanings, and the messages words convey.

There is beginning to be less reluctance to change from the known, traditional grammar to the idea that grammar is the study of the structure and system of language. The principle that the meanings of words are determined by the usage of those who speak the language is also being recognized. As the teacher adds linguistic terminology to his vocabulary and becomes skillful in approaching language analytically, his attitudes toward language and especially toward American English are being retrained.

This book is one educator's contribution toward meeting the need for interpretation of the linguistic literature to the elementary school teacher. It also seeks to make the teacher aware of the possibilities teaching our language has in the development of better speakers and writers.

GERTRUDE A. BOYD

PART ONE

Historical Background

Chapter 1

Language and English Grammar

LANGUAGE IS the most important form of human communication. Not only is language human, it is uniquely human and the key to all human activities. It is the vehicle through which the world can be understood and appreciated; without language, people are isolated and helpless.

As the major means of communication, language is essential to a communicating society. It is an intricate complex of patterns controlling the forms of words, of sentences, and of whole discourses. All these patterns are held together around a systematic core of patterns—the grammar of the language. Because of its central position, grammar is the key to the understanding of verbal communication.

Few subjects have had so ambiguous a place in American education as English grammar. Although the elementary school was once designated by the familiar term "grammar school," grammar is not a conspicuous subject area in the elementary school today. In prestige, it is probably near the bottom among the many subjects of the modern curriculum.

But grammar is being opened to new insights. Scholarship in

grammar is flourishing, both in the United States and abroad. Within the past quarter century significant advances have been made in becoming acquainted with the English language and how it works. Much greater progress seems likely in the next quarter century as scholars from many backgrounds pool their analyses of American English and other languages in an effort to set forth workable ideas for teaching and using language.

THE ORIGIN OF LANGUAGE

Everything human has grown out of an earlier form, and language is no exception; it grew from the calls and cries of animals. Human speech, however, enables the speaker to talk about experiences he has not actually had. Language is conditioned on memory and imagination and involves the ability to make a topic of conversation out of what one says.

According to Margaret Bryant and Janet Aiken, what may be called "prelanguage" consisted of meaningful cries used in context to express emotions, messages, commands, and other necessities of communication. Gradually words emerged, and they were combined and recombined to form first nonsentences and then sentences containing subjects and predicates. It is the nonsentence that retains most clearly the character of primitive speech.[1]

Speech-cries and words were combined and later differentiated into inflections and syntax. As many writers have pointed out, pronouns are clearly embedded in Latin and Hebrew, and Hebrew also shows prepositional and conjunctional affixes. In the early stages of grammar, every word has a potential inflection. It has only to prove itself useful in combination with numerous words until it loses its separate existence.

WHAT IS LANGUAGE?

A language is a set of symbols by which humans communicate. These symbols can be either spoken or written. To the grammarian, language is primarily a series of grammatical forms, roots, and endings. To the literary specialist, language is a series of words so arranged as to produce a harmonious or logical effect. To the lexicographer, language is fundamentally a list of words with their separate derivations, histories, and meanings. To the man in the street, language is what he uses to communicate with others.

There are many individuals interested in language—philosophers, psychologists, sociologists, anthropologists, linguists, and many others. Each group and individual defines language differently. The several definitions bring out different aspects of language which supplement rather than exclude one another. The definition used depends on the individual's point of view and interest at the time he makes his definition.

Language is a form of symbolism, and the group of symbols making up a language is systematic. It can also be said that all language has system in its sounds and in the way those sounds are put together. But sounds in themselves do not constitute language. It is only when the sounds are grouped into words, and the written signs into letters or significant symbols, that they begin to acquire the true character of language.

Hence, the word is a fundamental part of language. But the word by itself is an incomplete bearer of meaning. Just as the sequence of sounds completes the word, so the sequence of words completes the mental picture. Then a grammatical element is added to join the words. In this way language becomes a verbal, systematic symbolism which makes use of words and their arrangements to transmit information.

There are universals that appear in every language. All languages possess sounds, words and sequence of words, and grammatical form, or syntax. Every language has a pattern to which it adheres consistently.

Basic Assumptions of Language

Language includes both speech and writing, but in every civilization and in every person the vocal symbol system precedes the written symbol system. Speech reaches back to the origins of human society. People learn their language some years before they learn to read or write it. Writing, which has greater permanence and prestige, has a history of only about 7,000 years. All writing systems, however, are essentially representations of the forms of speech.

In defining language as a purely human activity, one linguist identifies the following characteristics:

1. Language is a set of sounds.
2. The connection between the sounds or sequences of sounds and the objects of the outside world is arbitrary and unpredictable.

3. Language is systematic.
4. Language is a set of symbols.
5. Language is complete.[2]

Why Analyze Language?

For human beings, language is a means of communication throughout their lives. They are so surrounded by language they tend to take its existence for granted. They do not usually analyze their use of language, except in the framework learned in school, and they tend to reject any innovation that goes beyond this. But today the lack of knowledge about American English—how it is spoken and written, how it is constructed, and how it functions—can no longer be ignored. This knowledge is of fundamental importance if teachers are to do a satisfactory job of teaching reading, spelling, and grammar and developing intelligent attitudes toward our language.

LINGUISTICS

Although linguistics is an old science, its modern experimental phase stressing the analysis of unwritten speech could be called one of the newest. As far as present knowledge goes, the science of linguistics was founded several centuries before Christ. Modern scientific linguistics was rediscovered in the early 19th century.

In considering what linguistics is, any definition depends on who is defining the word. For our purposes linguistics may be defined as a way of behaving in the attempt to discover information and to acquire knowledge about language. The information and knowledge that result from such inquiry behavior become part of what is meant by linguistics.

Linguistics is the scientific study of language. Since the study is scientific, the findings differ in a number of ways from traditional descriptions of language. In recent years there have been great advances in knowledge of the intricate structure of that most basic and wonderful of human inventions—language. As this knowledge has increased so has specific understanding of the history and structure of the English language.

A linguist uses scientific procedures to inquire into the role of language in human affairs. He investigates the phonology (sounds), morphology (word forms), and syntax (phrases and sentences) of language. He researches and examines language history, dialect geography (variations in language usage), usage (attitudes of certain speakers toward certain words and speakers), and semantics (the uses of language and the meanings of words).

Some people have difficulty at the beginning of language study in stripping off the preconceptions that have bound them to specific definitions and rules. Scientific investigation requires a mind open to new data and to looking at old data from all points of view.

During World War II linguists were asked to aid in teaching languages. Many of these specialists were committed to the primacy of speech over writing, since they were accustomed to starting from scratch in the study of a new language with only native informants. As linguists researched a new language, they emphasized teaching the spoken rather than the written language. But in carrying over linguistic principles into elementary and high schools, they discovered that the main emphasis was on learning to write the language, not on speaking it. This discovery was basic to the revolution in grammar that has affected attitudes, materials, and methods of teaching.

ORIGINS OF LINGUISTICS AND GRAMMAR

The origins of linguistics and English grammar are the same. Both grew out of the speculations of the Greeks. Both were transmitted through the Latin grammars of the medieval period and transformed during the Renaissance by the broadening interest in language. The divergence between linguistics and grammar came during the 18th and 19th centuries.

According to H. A. Gleason Jr., "There is a significant difference between the traditional grammarians and the 'linguists.' The two groups have tended to concentrate on different aspects of the problem. Traditional grammarians have inherited a framework for the structure of English. They have modified this whenever they have found it necessary to do so, but their chief attention has been focused on details of structure and usage. The linguists, on the other hand, have come to English with an interest more in the general theory of language and, in . . . the overall framework [of a language] than in the minor details. They have . . . tended to concentrate on the broader issues . . . central to the interests of the traditional grammarians. The results attained by the two groups are, therefore, largely complementary."[3]

As linguists extended their study they revealed that there are many different kinds of grammar. With the growth of the scientific method, language came under more rigorous scientific scrutiny. Linguists began to apply scientific techniques to many different languages, including English. Accelerated by the practical need for teaching languages during World War II, research into the nature of English grammar has moved rapidly in the past several decades.

GRAMMAR

The word "grammar" has many uses, some of them obsolete. It formerly referred to the whole body of writing, particularly classical writing in Latin and Greek. This meaning survives in the phrase "grammar school" to indicate a school where the curriculum includes elements of many things.

The grammar textbooks used in American schools through the 19th century often used the following definition: English grammar is the art of speaking and writing English correctly. Later in the century, a definition of grammar as "the science of language" came to be given more frequently by textbook writers. In this, they were following the almost universal practice of grammarians other than the authors of schoolbooks.[4]

But schoolbooks are used for a brief span, and individuals must understand how they communicate throughout their lifetime. This understanding requires insight into language that must be based, in part, on grammar. So grammar may be viewed not as a collection of rules but as a systematic core of patterns controlling the forms of words, of sentences, and of whole discourses. Thus grammar is a key to the understanding of verbal communication.

Usage and Grammar

Presumably there never has been a sharp distinction between usage and grammar. Often *usage* refers to the more specific details—rules applying to single words or phrases—or to the exceptional and marginal cases. *Grammar* refers to the more general features. Usage is the attitudes that speakers of a language have toward different aspects of their language—that is, certain pronunciations, words, and grammatical forms. It is also the study of the ways in which people actually use their language. The traditional school distinction between grammar and usage is an attempt at discrimination. The distinction is often fuzzy because the definitions of the two have been inexact and often inappropriate.

For many years the criterion for correctness used by certain grammarians has been usage. Joseph Priestley, for example, gave primacy to usage over authority. He says:

> It must be allowed that the custom of speaking is the original and only just standard of any language. We see, in all grammars, that this is sufficient to establish a rule, even contrary to the strongest analogies of the language with itself. Must not this custom, therefore, be allowed to have some weight, in favor of those forms of speech, to which our best writers and speakers seem evidently prone?[5]

In his grammar Priestley tried consistently to record what he had observed, refraining from judgments of absolute right and wrong.

But punctuation, words, and even grammatical forms change. What is good English today will not with any degree of certainty be good English tomorrow. To the speaker of English in the 1970s Old English seems practically a foreign language. Since language is in a constant state of flux, each person must learn to observe the language he uses and hears in order to know what good current English is.

Semantics and Grammar

Semantics, one of the most fascinating branches of language, is concerned in general with problems of meaning.

J. N. Hook and Michael G. Crowell describe semantics as a branch of lexicology and cite one of its definitions from Webster's Third New International Dictionary as: "The study dealing with the relations between signs and what they refer to, the relations between the signs of a system, and human behavior in reaction to signs including unconscious attitudes, influence of social institutions, and epistemological and linguistic assumptions." The part of this definition that is particularly rewarding, and not too abstruse for detailed development in the schools, is "human behavior in reaction to signs." The "signs" in question here are, of course, words.[6] Semantics is closely allied to the uses of language, such as determining meaning through use, relating grammar and meaning, and increasing vocabulary power.

Some of the earlier studies of semantics were concerned primarily with historical etymology. Today there are many interpretations and applications of semantics. One of the common assumptions is that two persons can never completely understand each other. No two persons have ever learned the same word under exactly the same circumstances; therefore each word has a special context for each individual. So communication at best is a compromise, for each person talks out of his own private world: his experiences, memories, and impressions.

THE TEACHER OF COMMUNICATION ARTS

A teacher of communication arts in the elementary school functions in several capacities. As rhetorician, he helps pupils learn how to put words together effectively, whether in writing or in speaking. As literary critic, he guides pupils to an appreciation of stories, poems, and drama, also improvised dramatizations. As grammarian, he leads pupils to discover how English words, phrases, and sentences are constructed.

An important factor in what is taught and how it is taught is the teacher's understanding of the books and other materials to be used in the classroom and their changing viewpoint from that of traditional grammar. This understanding must come about through self-education and through the study of linguistics, an acquaintance with the history of the English language, and the acquisition of a strong background in the "new" grammatical assumptions of language. New curricula are gradually evolving in textbooks and other materials and in methods courses in communication arts which will encompass the underlying linguistic patterns of grammar.

SUGGESTIONS AND ACTIVITIES FOR THE COLLEGE STUDENT AND THE CLASSROOM TEACHER

1. After reading this chapter and consulting other sources, make up your own definition of language. What sources can you find that agree with your definition? What sources disagree? Can you find areas of agreement?

2. What is good current English in your community? List at least 50 words or phrases that are commonly accepted locally. Would these words and phrases be accepted as standard English in any community?

3. What is your interpretation of the term "semantics"? How does your interpretation of semantics color your ideas of good current English?

4. Make several lists of words commonly used by class members. Let small groups discuss how they learned each of the words. Ask members to give their definitions of the words that have a special meaning for them because of the circumstances under which they learned the words—a memorable experience, a vivid impression.

5. A cry, a tonal inflection, or a gesture is a means of communication that is far more universal than language as it has been defined. They are in fact universal enough to be conveyed to animals as well as to other human beings. What other ways of communicating can you suggest that do not involve gesture or the understanding of words spoken?

6. The term "communication" includes more than the term "language," because communications may be and often are made by other than linguistic means. By what means are messages transmitted, other than by words? Does communication in "idea" units involve words used by the transmitter?

7. The duality of form and function runs throughout grammar. Some dualities are: (a) speaker and hearer, (b) writer and reader, and (c) speech and nonspeech communication. Discuss each of these in small groups. Give examples, with special reference to English grammar.

8. After reading the first chapter of Edward Sapir's *Language: An Introduction to the Study of Speech*,[7] discuss the relation between language and thought. Do you believe it is possible to think without speech?

9. If you have some acquaintanceship with a foreign language, list some of its grammatical differences from English. Do the rules of grammar for a language other than English enable you to use that language better than the rules of traditional grammar serve the English language?

NOTES

1. Margaret Bryant and Janet Aiken, *Psychology of English* (New York: Columbia University Press, 1940), pp. 33–35.

2. Archibald A. Hill, *Introduction to Linguistic Structures* (New York: Harcourt Brace Jovanovich, Inc., 1958), pp. 3–7.

3. H. A. Gleason, Jr., "What Grammar?" *Harvard Educational Review,* 34 (1964): 273–74. Copyright © 1964 by President and Fellows of Harvard College.

4. H. A. Gleason, Jr., *Linguistics and English Grammar* (New York: Holt, Rinehart & Winston, Inc., 1965), p. 7.

5. Joseph Priestley, *The Rudiments of English Grammar,* 2d ed. (London: R. Griffiths, 1761), Preface. Quoted in Albert C. Baugh, *A History of the English Language,* 2d ed., 1957 p. 341.

6. J. N. Hook and Michael G. Crowell, *Modern English Grammar for Teachers* (New York: Ronald Press Co., 1970), p. 12. Copyright © 1970 The Ronald Press Company, New York.

7. Edward Sapir, *Language: An Introduction to the Study of Speech.* (New York: Harcourt, Brace & World, Inc., 1921).

Chapter 2

The English Language

NO LANGUAGE IS the same at its end as it was at its beginning, and no language is spoken in precisely the same form throughout the entire area in which it is used. Languages are continually undergoing changes; their current status is an outgrowth of previous stages of development. English, like all other languages, is subject to the constant processes of growth and decay that characterize all forms of life.

Even as recently as the time of Shakespeare, English usage was so different from today's that Shakespearean grammar provides a special field of study. Much of the vocabulary of Old English has been lost. The development of new words to meet new conditions is one of the most familiar phenomena of our language.

The migratory habits of man provide the need for the development of new words or speech habits as the inhabitants of one group mingle with another across a river or a mountain range. The change that is constantly going on in a living language can be most easily seen in its vocabulary. Old words die out, new words are added, and existing words change their meaning. Less obvious, perhaps, but also evident to the observer and user are changes in pronunciation.

THE INDO-EUROPEAN FAMILY OF LANGUAGES

Philologists divide the leading languages of the world into families. English belongs to the Indo-European family, which is one of the most significant, both in geographical extent and number of users. According to Margaret Bryant, the Indo-European language system is divided into nine groups: Indian, Iranian, Armenian, Hellenic, Albanian, Italic, Celtic, Balto-Slavonic, and Germanic or Teutonic.

These nine branches have certain features in common. They are all inflectional, designating syntactical distinctions such as case, number, gender, tense, and voice by varying the form of a word. For instance, in English we generally indicate the plural of a noun by adding -*s* to the singular (*boy, boys*) and form the present participle by adding -*ing* to the present tense (*go, going*). Another feature of the Indo-European family is the common word stock, comprised of a number of words not found in other types of languages and formed with similar methods of pronunciation. For example, it is not difficult to observe that Sanskrit *tri,* Persian *thri,* Greek *treis,* Latin *tres,* Celtic *tri,* Slavonic *tri,* Lithuanian *tri,* Gothic *thri,* German *drei,* Icelandic *thriu,* Dutch *drie,* English *three* all come from a single original root.[1]

BEGINNINGS OF THE ENGLISH TONGUE

The English language as a separate and distinct entity began in about the fifth century, but it was not until the beginning of the seventh that the language definitely emerged from the confusion and turmoil of the conquest of Britain and began to take its place among the nascent modern tongues of Europe. Its strengths and its weaknesses, its complex grammatical structure, its hardy, earthy vocabulary, its harsh rugged sounds, and its unrefined yet miraculously expressive syntax all go to form the backbone of the tongue spoken in America, Britain, and the Dominions today.

The development of a language is a continuous process, and English is no exception. Its history can be traced through three stages: Old English, Middle English, and Modern English. Old English is known as a language full of inflections, Middle English as a language of leveled inflections, and Modern English as a language of lost inflections. There have been few losses of inflections since 1600, the chief ones being the gradual disappearance of the forms of the subjunctive mood and the limited use of *ye, thou, thee, thy,* and *thine.*

These uses can still be found in literature but rarely, if ever, are they heard in speech.

The English spoken today is not the fruit of a deliberate human design. It is the result of a long series of historical events and the influence of many branches of the Indo-European language system.

Influence of Celtic

Before recorded history the British Isles had been visited, overrun, and conquered by two separate groups of Celtic invaders, speaking tongues that were the remote ancestors of present-day Gaelic and Welsh. The first identified language in England is that of the Celts; Celtic is the first Indo-European tongue known to have been used in the British Isles. The influence of Celtic was slight, with place names—Kent, Dundee, Avon, Dover—and such words as *binn* for *basket* or *crib,* and *bratt* for *cloak* the most evident examples. Less than 20 words can be identified in the English language today as having been derived from Celtic influence.

Influence of Latin

The Latin influence was somewhat stronger than the Celtic. The tendency was to translate borrowed ideas into English instead of borrowing words, as later became the practice. Old English vocabulary was enriched by a number of direct loans from Latin. It has been estimated that the number of loan words from Latin before 1050 was about 400. This influence was mainly upon the learned language and not on everyday speech.

Flourishing trade with Roman merchants continued the borrowing which had begun long ago on the Continent when Germanic tribes first encountered traders from the Mediterranean. The borrowings of such words as *cheese, cup, kettle, wine, wall* and place names such as Lancaster, Gloucester, Winchester were due to the contact the Anglo-Saxons had with Roman merchants on the Continent. The Roman missionaries who introduced Christianity into England in 597 also brought a number of direct transfers from the Latin language. Among the words added were *abbot, candle, hymn, organ, psalm, synod, temple.*

Classical Latin has not changed in more than 2,000 years, and when a language ceases to change it is classed as a dead language.

English remains subject to growth, change, and decay, the characteristics of a living language.

OLD ENGLISH PERIOD

The Old English, or Anglo-Saxon, period began with the coming of the Jutes, Angles, and Saxons into England about the middle of the fifth century. There were no written documents in the Anglo-Saxon or Old English of the first few hundred years. The tongues spoken by these groups were closely related, but they did give rise to somewhat divergent Old English dialects as the groups settled in the various sections of Britain.

Once the language of the Anglo-Saxons began to be written and to be studied along with Latin, it was brought into contact with the wide currents of world culture still pulling strongly from Rome. The language of the first significant literature in English dates from the late seventh century. Traces of the Saxon dialects are distinguishable in the provincial speech of English today.

The Germanic settlers who brought their language with them left behind on the continental North Sea coast less venturesome members of the tribe whose tongue in due time turned into Frisian. This language is so close to English that the following rhyme can still be understood, at least in part, by modern English speakers:

> Bred, butter en grene chiese,
> En wat dat net sayse ken
> Is kin uprjuchte Friese.

> Bread, butter and green cheese,
> And who cannot say that
> Is no upright Frisian.[2]

Today Frisian is spoken by a few thousand individuals in Holland and on the nearby islands of the North Sea. Some scholars have held that Old Frisian and Old English were originally one speech. Frisian is the language most nearly akin to English.

After Christianity was established in Britain, schools, books, and the art of writing followed. Alfred the Great (871–899) became the inspiration for this movement. Most of the prose in West Saxon and the poetry, mainly Anglian, was copied by West Saxon scribes, whose transcriptions have been preserved.

The language spoken by King Alfred was West Saxon, a dialect of Old English. It can be compared to Modern German in respect to declensions, for in both there are nouns with four cases in the singular and plural. Both languages show a large number of verbs (called "strong") that indicate changes in tense by internal vowel change. There are also constant relations in the sound patterns. Minor changes in both languages have obscured some of the clear correspondences between the two.

The influence of the dialects brought by the Anglo-Saxons was affected by the enthusiastic and intense study of classical writers during this period. This study made Old English authors conscious of style and sentence structure in their own language.

Danish Influence

Progress in language growth under the Anglo-Saxons was cut short with the Danish invasion at the end of the eighth century when monastic schools and manuscripts were destroyed. Later the Danes began adapting themselves to the ways of English life. Though they were pagan worshipers of Woden and other Teutonic gods, many of them accepted Christianity.

In some places the Scandinavians gave up their language quite early; in others Danish remained for some time the customary language. However, with frequent intermarriage between the two races and the similarity between the two tongues, a considerable number of people were to some degree bilingual.

The Danes contributed many homely and practical loanwords to the English vocabulary. Many common words such as *man, wife, father, mother, house* were the same in both Old English and the Scandinavian language.

A simple criterion for identifying loanwords is by certain sounds. One of the easiest to recognize is the sound of *sk*. In Old English this was early palatalized to *sh* (written *sc*), except possibly in the combination *scr*, whereas in the Scandinavian countries it retained its hard sound. Native words like *ship, shall, fish* have *sh* in Modern English. Words borrowed from the Scandinavian are generally still pronounced with sk: *sky, skin, skill, scrape, scrub, bask, whisk.* The development of the *g* and *k* in words like *give, get, egg, kid* is also Scandinavian.[3]

The plural forms of pronouns—*they, their, them*—were acquired from the Scandinavian influence, which gradually displaced the Old English forms. These are a great acquisition to English, since without them the plural and singular forms of *he* would sound almost exactly alike. Stuart Robertson and F. G. Cassidy state that "Aside from Greek, Latin, and French, only Danish has made a really substantial contribution to the English vocabulary."[4]

More than 1,400 places in England, largely in the North and East, have Scandinavian names. Among these are the place names adding *-by*, the Danish word for "town," as in Derby, Rugby, Grimsby; those adding *-thorp* for "village," as in Althorp, Linthorpe; those adding *-thwaite* for "an isolated piece of ground," as in Applethwaite; and those adding *-toft* for "a messuage" (a dwelling house with adjacent buildings and adjoining lands), as in Eastoft and Nortoft.

Scandinavian also left its mark on English in its extensive use of verbs with adverb-prepositions of the type combining *take* with *up, down, in, out, off, on, from, to*. These forms were commonly used in Middle and Elizabethan English, but they were later scorned by the classicists and condemned outright by Samuel Johnson, who published the *Dictionary of the English Language* in 1755. The use of such terms has multiplied exceedingly in recent years.

The Anglo-Saxon writers frequently coined words for abstract learned concepts out of simple forms already existent in their own language. They did this by translating literally the elements of the Latin words. Thus the Old English vocabulary was increased under Roman inspiration without sacrifice of native ingredients.

By the end of the Old English period, England had a recognized literary language which had been used for several hundred years for important creative and translated writings. By the year 1000 certain changes were beginning to affect the literary language. The multiplicity of endings was gradually being reduced, and cases originally kept distinct were beginning to fall together with identical terminations.

An examination of Old English shows that some of the words are almost the same as those used today. Others have undergone considerable change, and still others have vanished. In Old English, word order was much less fixed than it is today. Spelling was much more phonetic; in general, there were no silent letters. In pronunciation, vowel sounds were more similar to those found in modern continental languages than those in Modern English; and consonant sounds were not much different from those of Modern English. Punctuation marks other than periods were rare.

Relationship of English and German

Many German and English words are practically identical, not because one is derived from or borrowed from the other, for the borrowings are few, but because they had their beginnings in a common source known as Primitive Germanic. The differences between English and German arose because each language followed its own course and was exposed to particular influences throughout the centuries of its growth.

Consonants have undergone a change that belongs to the High German language alone. English *p* generally appears in the literary German of today as *f* or *pf* (*ship, Schiff; pipe, Pfeife*); English *d* as German *t* (*cold, kalt; deep, tief*); English *v* as German *b* in cognates (*over, ober; knave, Knabe*); and *t* often as German *z* or *tz* (*to, zu; ten, zehn; sit, sitzen; cat, Katze*). Because of the great inflectional leveling that has gone on in English, the inflection of literary German is much less like that of Modern English than that of Old English or traditional German, both of which usually expressed new ideas in native terms. Modern English is more like the Low German of northern Germany. This similarity can be noted in Modern English *deep, heart,* which are Low German *deep, Hart.* English and Dutch have the same word, *water,* and others that differ very little, as *twenty, twintig; wife, wyf.*

Although English has radically changed its forms and structure (being influenced to a great extent by Latin and French in particular) and has borrowed words from many languages, it is basically a Germanic tongue.

MIDDLE ENGLISH HERITAGE

Throughout the Old English or Anglo-Saxon period the language was constantly changing. During the last few years of this period the Norman French, who spoke a provincial French dialect, began infiltrating Britain. When the Norman armies landed on English soil in 1066 their language had actually preceded them. Throughout the Middle English period, which extends to about 1500, the French influence led to gradual modification of English law, language, and social custom. The Normans continued to speak French, and learning French was compulsory for those children of the English who attended school. Most of the native speakers, who spoke English, became necessarily illiterate and remained so for several generations.

While the English language was neglected and uncorrected by formal writing or extensive reading, it tended to change more rapidly in this period than it had previously. It lost almost all of its words derived from literature and other vocabulary primarily from written sources. The leveling of forms produced a greatly simplified grammar. Many of the distinctions of Old English were lost in the process.

When two languages exist side by side for a long time, as did French and English in England, many words are transferred from one language to the other, especially to the one in the inferior position. So it was with English, which borrowed a large number of words from the French, enough to change the general character of the language from unilingual to bilingual.

As English became influenced by the Romance languages as well as by the Teutonic, it developed into a language made up of two merging strains. Never before or since has English taken in so many words, phrases, and idioms. Many of these took the place of English words. French pronunciations and spellings also came in at this time. For instance, the introduction of *u* after *g* to indicate the hard *g* accounts for Modern English *tongue* from Old English *tunge;* it also accounts for spellings like *guest, guilt, guild, language.*

Old English sentences had used the inverted order and delayed clausal verbs that can be found in Modern German. With the reduction of Old English declensions, the English sentence fell increasingly into the word order habitual today: subject, predicate, complement. Changes in grammar also occurred:

> Almost all nouns were attracted into the declension represented by *stan,* with the plural ending in *-as* later weakened into the ending *-es.* Only a few survived in the other declensions. The vowels of unaccented endings were reduced to the obscure sound [ə], written *-e-.* The verbs retained endings not unlike those current in the time of King Alfred. The adjectives retained vestiges of inflection, even slightly differentiating strong forms from weak; but the elaborate declensions of Old English adjectives were forgotten. The reduction of endings to short, unstressed syllables gave the language a trochaic and dactylic effect.[5]

Grammar was only one aspect of the change. The pronunciation shifted, and the alteration in vocabulary was particularly far-reaching, with thousands of French and Latin terms added to the word stock. The whole pattern of the language was modified. The Norman Conquest did not account for all these changes, but it did do so for many of them.

As the pronunciation shifted, combining the French accentuation on the last syllable and the English on the first, a wavelike rise and fall of stress was produced. This can be noted in the French importations with a strong secondary stress retained on the last syllable: *rê-ve-rèn-ce, dô-mi-nâ-ci-oùn.* Out of these divergent sources came the iambic-trochaic movements of English which Chaucer used so brilliantly in his narrative verse.

In the court established by the Normans both clergy and nobility knew and spoke only French and Latin. But English, the language of the subject population, lived on without formal schooling and literature. Thus by the beginning of the 13th century there was a trilingual England in which French, Latin, and English existed side by side, each for a different purpose and with a different function. The first was the literary and courtly tongue, the second the language of the church and legal documents, and the third the tongue of common intercourse.

The churchly writers in the latter 12th century were schooled primarily in Latin and Norman French. These men adapted the spelling of the upper-class languages to the native idiom, trying to write phonetically what they actually heard. Thus English reemerged as a literary language before 1400.

French and English Words

Through the Norman rulers and landlords all sorts of French words came into English. There were words to do with government: *parliament, majesty, alliance, tax, government;* church words: *parson, sermon, baptism, incense, crucifix, religion;* words for foods: *veal, beef, mutton, bacon, jelly, peach, lemon, cream, biscuit;* colors: *blue, scarlet, vermilion;* household words: *curtain, chair, lamp, blanket, parlor;* play words: *dance, chess, music, leisure, conversation;* literary words: *story, romance, poet, literary;* learned words: *study, logic, grammar, noun, surgeon, anatomy, stomach;* just ordinary words of all sorts: *nice, very, second, age, bucket, gentle, final, fault, flower, cry, count, sure, move, surprise, plain.*[6]

Over a period of more than 100 years many people must have used as many French words as English words in their speech, but English remained English in sound structure and in grammar. Most of the high-frequency words—pronouns, prepositions, conjunctions, auxiliaries—as well as a great many ordinary nouns, verbs, and adjectives were not replaced by borrowings.

The stream of French words that began to enter English in 1066 is still unbroken today. By 1250 about a thousand French words had entered the language, mostly of the kind that the lower classes would naturally acquire from the nobility: *baron, noble, dame, servant, messenger, feast, story, rime, lay.*

Perhaps one of the most notable results of the Norman French invasion for the English language was the creation of the many synonyms that distinguish English to this day, giving it a firm foothold in both the Germanic and the Romance fields. As early as 1225 a devotional work showed such double forms as *cheritie* and *luve, bigamie* and *twiewifing;* Chaucer speaks later of *cure* and *hele, lord* and *sire;* Caxton of *awreke* and *avenge, olde* and *auncyent, glasse* and *mirrour;* and the Book of Common Prayer has to this day *acknowledge* and *confess, dissemble* and *cloke, assemble* and *meet, pray* and *beseech, perceive* and *know, power* and *might.*[7]

During the centuries of Norman domination the English language was altered in almost every way. The Normans found English a synthetic, highly inflected language like Greek, Latin, and Modern German, but when they had finished putting their imprint upon it, it was an analytic language, with rapidly disappearing inflections, like Modern French. Near the end of the 14th century a written language developed which was accepted generally in the 15th century and became the standard speech.

Influence of the Printing Press

One of the greatest influences exerted on the English language has been the printing press, introduced in England in 1476 by William Caxton. The role of Caxton was more in the fixation than in the formation of the language. Through his utilization of Gutenberg's invention, the works of Chaucer, Gower, Lydgate, and Mallory were made accessible to the English reading public. Caxton's great work lay in the standardization of spelling. The word seen in print is indelibly impressed upon the mind of the reader. Thus the printed form exerted influence upon the spoken tongue, and English became a full-blown cultural tongue utilized by many speakers, writers, and readers.

Manuscript books began to disappear as movable type came into use. By 1640, more than 20,000 titles had appeared in English, including all types of books, from mere pamphlets to massive folios. Books began to be available for all rather than an expensive luxury of the few. Moreover, it was now possible to reproduce many copies of a book, all exactly alike. This was a powerful force for promoting a standard, uniform language.

Before the printing press, there was no authority for the language, so it continued to evolve in its basic feature, morphology. The spread of the printed word arrested this evolutionary process of language, which some view as deplorable, others as desirable. But there continued to be growth of individual words, with their semantic burdens and endless possibilities for combinations. The extension of trade enlarged the English vocabulary by words drawn from every part of the world. The exchange of both commodities and ideas is stimulating to language.

The printing press had a tremendous effect upon English in making it more uniform and in standardizing it. This force was multiplied by the increased interest in education that began in the later Middle Ages and has continued ever since. Popular education has enabled the printing press to have an influence upon language and thought that is almost too powerful to describe. Although the language employed throughout Europe by educated people was Latin, the popular demand of the people in England to read and speak English brought about the writing of books in all fields of knowledge in that language.

MODERN ENGLISH

Of all the things that have happened to English, the reduction of inflectional endings and the increased inflexibility of word order have been most important in giving the language its modern characteristics. Although these changes were not completed in the Middle English period and will never be completed while the language lives, they were far advanced by the year 1500, a date chosen rather arbitrarily as the beginning of Modern English.

Between the years 1500 and 1700, many of the traits that characterize the language today developed. The study of the classics stressed during the Renaissance meant a strong influence of Latin and Greek on English, marked by the borrowing of words and style from such authors as Cicero and Vergil. Some writers translated Greek works into Latin; others translated Latin and Greek works into English.

But there was a conservative reaction against "improving" the mother tongue. Some groups believed their language should depend upon its own resources. Both movements enriched the language; one by borrowing and imitating, the other by developing its own resources. For example, few letters were written in English before 1400, French and Latin being viewed as the normal media of correspondence. After the middle of the 15th century, however, public writings and statutes of Parliament began to be written in English.

DIFFICULTIES IN ACQUIRING FACILITY IN ENGLISH

One of the difficulties the foreign student encounters in learning English is that very simplification of inflections which is considered among its assets. All languages have their special ways of saying things, but speakers of other languages complain of the difficulty of expressing themselves in English not only logically but idiomatically. An idiom is a form of expression peculiar to one language. The distinction between *My husband isn't up yet* and *My husband isn't down yet,* or the quite contradictory uses of *fast* in *go fast* and *stand fast,* seem to the speaker of another language to be without reasonable justification.

One of the more serious criticisms of English is the chaotic character of its spelling and its frequent lack of correlation between spelling and pronunciation. Writing is merely a mechanical means of recording speech. Theoretically, the most adequate system of spelling is the one that best combines simplicity and consistency. In English the vowel sound in *believe, receive, leave, machine, be, see* is in each case represented by a different spelling.

One cannot tell how to spell an English word by its pronunciation or how to pronounce it by its spelling. The English-speaking child spends valuable time during the early years of his education learning to spell his own language.

ADVANTAGES OF THE ENGLISH LANGUAGE

The English language is occupying an increasingly prominent place in international communication. Chief among the advantages of the English language is the mixed character of its vocabulary. English is classified as a Teutonic language, that is, it belongs to the group of languages to which German, Dutch, Flemish, Danish, Swedish, and Norwegian also belong. It shares with these languages similar grammatical structure and many common words. Nevertheless, more than half of its vocabulary is derived from Latin, and it shares a great number of words with those languages of Europe that are derived from Latin, notably French, Italian, Spanish, and Portuguese.

English has grammatical simplicity, a mark of progress in language. The evolution of language is a story of progressive simplification, and in this English has gone further than any other language in Europe. Inflections in the noun as spoken have been reduced to a sign of the plural and a form for the possessive case. The complicated agreements that make German difficult are absent from English.

Commerce and colonization carried on by those who speak English have spread the language throughout the world, so that it is used or understood in some form by vast numbers of people. English has shown itself to be a cosmopolitan speech in that it is ready to adopt a term from any other language if it proves to represent a useful idea. As long as Englishmen and Americans play an important part in world affairs, their language will continue to grow in use among other nations.

English enjoys an exceptional advantage over all other European languages in having adopted *natural* in place of *grammatical gender*. In European languages it is necessary to know the gender along with the meaning of every noun. This need was stripped away in English during the Middle English period, and today the gender of every noun is known, since it is determined by meaning. All nouns naming living creatures are masculine or feminine, according to the sex of the individual, and all other nouns are neuter. Attributive gender, as of a ship as feminine, sun and moon as masculine or feminine, is personification and a matter of rhetoric, not grammar.

The English language today reflects many centuries of development. Among the factors influencing a common language and a common vocabulary are the rise of an important middle class and the growth of commerce and industry, as well as the advances of science and printing procedures. Each in its own way has contributed to the English language.

Thus English has passed through three periods of development—Old English, Middle English, and Modern English. American English is usually considered to be the latest stage of Modern English.

SUGGESTIONS AND ACTIVITIES FOR THE COLLEGE STUDENT AND THE CLASSROOM TEACHER

1. How can you account for the core of functioning English vocabulary as being Anglo-Saxon? These words include common names for things like *word* and *neighbor;* words for customary actions like *go* and *speak;* words which have little meaning in themselves but are essential in holding the English language together, like *a, the, of, from, get, do, had, there.*
2. New words and new meanings for words are added to the language both by specialization and by generalization. One meaning of a word leads to another meaning. Some meanings disappear. A change in society creates a demand for new words; new words are formed by juggling old ones. Can you take a word such as *tap,* meaning to draw liquor out of a barrel by means of a bung-stop, and illustrate various meanings from history, literature, politics, or just common usage?
3. Language must have not only flexibility to live and grow but currency to be understood and stability. Without stability you might never learn to speak, because the language could be changing faster than you were able to learn it. Do you feel that the English language is changing faster in the 1970s than it was in the 1920s? To what do you attribute this rapid change?
4. Can you imagine a world in which the language was changing faster than all of the inhabitants could learn it? What other changes would be taking place? In the early history of the English language, were the many languages brought in by the invaders of England introduced at a faster pace than they could be absorbed by the general population?
5. The words *emotive* and *emotional* have been used by some speakers with a common meaning, but *emotional* means not only given to emotion but also, like *emotive,* appealing to the emotions. Modern usage, however, has differentiated the words usefully by

assigning *emotive* to the cause and *emotional* to the effect (see H. W. Fowler, *A Dictionary of Modern Usage,* 2d, ed., 1965). The emotive use of language is directed primarily to move others to action. Such comments as "My country, right or wrong" obtain results. Can you cite the uses of emotive and emotional language in social and political situations and in legal cases?

6. There are many likenesses in the speech habits of people inhabiting a particular region at a particular time. But what constitutes a language? What differences do you find between a language and a dialect?

7. Grimm's Law, a linguistic principle, has helped linguists in grouping the Germanic languages. This principle pertains to a shift in consonants, as *fish* in English is *pisce* in Latin, and *foot* is *pedes. Mother* in English is *mater* in Latin, *father* is *pater,* and *brother* is *frater.* This is true of hundreds of words having similar characteristics. Where *f* occurs in English you may expect to find *p* in Latin, and where *wh* occurs in English you may expect to find *t* in Latin (Charlton Laird, *The Miracle of Language,* Fawcett World Library, 1963). What other common characteristics of the Germanic languages can you discover? What is the importance of Grimm's law and other such linguistic principles in studying languages?

8. Compare the attitude of the 18th century toward adding loan words from other languages and that of the 20th century. Can you cite newspapers or periodicals which have taken a stand on using words from other languages to express ideas commonly viewed as typical American?

NOTES

1. Margaret M. Bryant, *Modern English and Its Heritage,* 2d ed. (New York: The Macmillan Co., 1962), pp. 10–12.

2. Mario Pei, *The Story of English* (Greenwich, Conn.: Fawcett Publications, Inc., 1952), p. 11.

3. Otto Jespersen, *Growth and Structure of the English Language,* 9th ed. (New York: Free Press, 1968); cited in Bryant, *Modern English and Its Heritage,* p. 37.

4. Stuart Robertson and F. G. Cassidy, *The Development of Modern English,* 2d ed. (New York: Prentice-Hall, Inc., 1954), p. 41.

5. Margaret Schlauch, *The Gift of Language* (New York: Dover Publications, Inc., 1955), p. 206.

6. Paul Roberts, *Understanding English* (New York: Harper & Bros., 1958.)

7. Pei, *Story of English,* pp. 41–42.

Chapter 3

The English Language in America

In 1500 ENGLISH was a minor language spoken by a few people on a small island. Now it is perhaps the greatest language of the world, spoken natively by over a quarter of a billion people and as a second language by many millions more. When one speaks of English, he must specify whether he means American English, British English, Australian English, Indian English, or whatever, since the differences are considerable.

An American cannot go to England or an Englishman to America confident that he will always understand and be understood. The earliest changes in the English language in America, distinguishing it from the language of the mother country, were in the vocabulary. The English speak of *lorry (truck)*, *windscreen (windshield)*, *bonnet (hood)*, *petrol (gasoline* or *gas)*, *cinema (movie)*, *wireless (radio)*. But there are many more likenesses than differences in the English spoken in England and that spoken in America. Generally speaking, when an American word expresses an idea in a way that appeals to the English as fitting or effective, the word or expression is ultimately adopted in England.

If you were asked to define American English, the language you use, your reply might be "All the words and sentences used to express my thoughts." Long practice in situations has made plain what is meant by expressions in American English.

CHARACTERISTICS OF AMERICAN ENGLISH

The characteristics chiefly noted in American English are: (1) its general uniformity throughout the country; (2) its impatient disregard for grammatical, syntactical, and phonological rule and precedent; and (3) its large capacity for taking in new words and phrases from outside sources and for manufacturing words out of its own materials. American English is a speech for the whole nation. No other country can show such linguistic solidarity. The dialects of the counties in England have such marked differences that it is doubtful whether a Lancashire miner and a Lincolnshire farmer could understand each other. Americans can be proud that this country has, strictly speaking, only one language.

There are some regional peculiarities in pronunciation and intonation today, but when it comes to words habitually used and the way they are used, all Americans follow virtually the same pattern. A Boston taxi driver could go to work in Chicago or San Francisco without running any risk of misunderstanding his new fares. Once he has flattened his *a*'s a bit and picked up a few dozen localisms, he would be, to all linguistic intents and purposes, fully naturalized.

The American views linguistics as a means of making his language as he goes along. A novelty that meets the national fancy for the terse, the vivid, the bold, the imaginative may be widely accepted. H. L. Mencken points out that many new verbs have been fashioned by the simple process of prefixing the preposition to common nouns: *to dicker, to cord* (wood), *to style, to author.* Others arose as metaphors, as *to whitewash* (figuratively) and *to squat* (on unoccupied land). Some were made by hitching suffixes to nouns, as *to deputize, to infract.* Some verbs seem to have been produced by onomatapoeia: *to fizzle, to tote.* An endless series of verb phrases—*to draw a bead, to face the music, to take to the woods, to fly off the handle, to go on the warpath*—all are products of pioneer life. *Handy, chunky, solid* (in the sense of well-to-do), *underpinned,* and *cute* were already secure in Revolutionary days. Meanings of common words were also changed by the colonists: *to haul* (to move by force or violence) to *to transport in a vehicle* and *to heft* (to lift up) to *to weigh by lifting.*[1]

Seventeenth-century English differed from its modern counterpart in many aspects of speech. Although the language had in general developed most of the inflections which are used in present-day English—the noun plurals, the objective form *them* in the plural pronoun, the past tense and past participle forms of the weak verb—a few interesting earlier features remained. Among these were the double forms of the pronoun of address: *thou, ye,* and *you.* The use of these was governed in part by considerations of social rank and in part on the basis of emotional overtones. The Quakers, committed to a belief in the innate equality of all men, interpreted the duality of the pronoun of address as a negation of that equality and argued a return to an older state of the language where the two forms were differentiated solely on the basis of number. The double supply of pronouns was accompanied by a difference in verb structure—*thou teachest* but *ye* or *you teach.* After the *thou* form fell into disfavor, so too did the verb inflections ending in -*est,* leaving the second person singular of the verb identical with the first person and with all forms of the plural.[2]

THE LANGUAGE OF THE COLONISTS

The English language was brought to America by colonists from England who settled along the Atlantic seaboard in the 17th century. The language of the colonists had been greatly influenced by the literary standard which had arisen in the vicinity of London and had come to be accepted in most parts of England. The English colonists in the New World were speaking Elizabethan English—the language of Shakespeare, Milton, Lyly, Marlowe, and Lodge—when they came to America.

There was great similarity in the language spoken by Smith's Virginians, Calvert's Marylanders, the Plymouth fathers, the Bostonians of the Massachusetts Bay Colony, Roger Williams' Rhode Islanders, and Penn's Quakers. But the language spoken sounded somewhat different from its 20th-century counterpart. The differences that exist today between American and British English must either have taken place in American English after the colonists settled on this continent or have occurred in British English after the emigrants left their homeland. Or there may have been changes in both divisions of the language after the period of settlement.

Thus it was the early colonists who brought the English language to America and established its form. Those who came later were largely assimilated in a generation or two. Though their influence may have been felt, it is difficult to define.

The point of view that American English is different and separate from British English has been held from the time of the American Revolution, when a definite national consciousness was being established. After the signing of the Declaration of Independence, the person who did most in furthering the idea of a separate American language was Noah Webster, who compiled a spelling book, grammar, and reader. His treatment of questions of language and his *American Dictionary of the English Language* (1828) were especially influential. In the preface to this significant work he says:

> It is not only important, but, in a degree necessary, that the people of this country, should have an *American Dictionary of the English Language;* for, although the body of the language is the same as in England and it is desirable to perpetuate that sameness, yet some differences must exist. Language is the expression of ideas; and if the people of our country cannot preserve an identity of ideas, they cannot retain an identity of language. Now an identity of ideas depends materially upon a sameness of things or objects with which the people of the two countries are conversant. But in no two portions of the earth, remote from each other, can such identity be found. Even physical objects must be different. But the principal differences between the people of this country and of all others, arise from different forms of government, different laws, institutions and customs . . . . No person in this country will be satisfied with the English definitions of the words *congress, senate* and *assembly, court,* etc. for although these are words used in England, yet they are applied in this country to express ideas which they do not express in that country.[3]

INFLUENCE OF EUROPEAN IMMIGRANTS

There were three great periods of immigration to this country from Europe which influenced the development of American English. The first extends from the settlement of Jamestown, Virginia in 1607 to the end of colonial times. About two-thirds of the earliest settlers around Massachusetts Bay came from the southeastern counties of England—many from East Anglia, which was the principal center of

Puritanism in England. Therefore a basically southeastern English type of speech prevailed in Massachusetts.

By the time the 13 original colonies had ratified the federal Constitution, there were about four million English-speaking people in America, most of them east of the Appalachian Mountains. From the linguistic point of view this was the first and most decisive stage in the history of the English language in the United States, which by universal consent but less accurately is called American English.

The second period covers the expansion of the original 13 colonies west of the Appalachians and the arrival of immigrants from the British Isles, Holland, and Germany. Colonists spread throughout New England and the Middle Atlantic states.

The middle colonies were settled by people whose speech was native to the north and west of England, the Scotch-Irish, and by Germans. From these groups there developed a speech area termed the Midland, separating North from South. In the Midland area of the South Atlantic states the r sound is retained in *farm, board, door, father,* and the like, as in the English spoken in Northern Britain, though it has been considerably weakened.

The Midland is also set off from other regions by its use of certain words, usually having to do with the house and farm and invariably simple and homely. It is more sharply differentiated from the North in this respect than in pronunciation. Northern *pail* and *faucet* are in the Midland *bucket* and *spicket* (*spigot*), respectively. *Skillet* is primarily a regional word of the Midland, though it has spread elsewhere; in the North and in a large part of the coastal South the utensil is usually called a *spider,* though the trade name *frying pan* may be heard in towns and cities all over the country. Midland cows are called by shouting *sook* or *sookie;* in the North the call is *boss, co-boss, comeboss, co,* or *coaf;* in the South it is *co-wench, co-inch,* or *co-ee.* The construction *I want in* (or *out* or *off*) is (according to the records of the *Linguistic Atlas of the United States and Canada*) in frequent use in the Midland area, though avoided by educated speakers. This construction is not a Pennsylvania Germanism. It occurs in older English and was presumably transmitted to this country in the northern English speech of the Scotch-Irish, who subsequently carried it with them in their western migrations.[4]

The South Atlantic settlements were sparsely populated. The Virginia settlers were a motley group of Royalists, blackguards, political refugees, Commonwealth soldiers, deported prisoners, indentured servants, and many Puritans. More than half of the colonists were from the southern part of England, so a type of speech basically southeastern English was to prevail here. Shortly after the middle of the 18th century emigrants from Virginia and the Carolinas moved into Georgia and the cotton lands of the Gulf states. In the lands beyond the Appalachians to the south, other migrations were taking place. Virginians, Marylanders, Pennsylvanians, and North Carolinians settled in large numbers in Kentucky. Scotch-Irish from the southern mountain country joined the French in Louisiana; some of them pushed westward from the Appalachians to the Ozarks; some came as far as eastern Texas.

The *third* period took place during the closing decades of the 19th century, when a million Scandinavians settled in America for the most part in Minnesota and the upper Mississippi Valley. They were followed by millions of Czechs, Slovaks, Poles, Yugoslavs, and Italians. The cosmopolitan character of the United States was accentuated by the attachment of French and Spanish populations in the South and West, the presence of native Indian tribes in the Middle West, and the absorption of the Chinese and Japanese who penetrated the Pacific Coast and the African Negroes who were brought to the Atlantic Coast. At no time was there danger that English might not be capable of completely assimilating any immigrant tongue.

ARCHAIC FEATURES IN AMERICAN ENGLISH

Over the years American English has continued to preserve some features of the various periods of the development of the English language which have gone out of use in the standard speech of England. American English pronunciation has qualities that were characteristic of the English speech of the 17th and 18th centuries, for example the flat *a* in *fast, path, dance, can't, half, grass.* At the end of the 18th-century southern England began to change from what is called a flat *a* to a broad *a* in these words, that is from a sound like the *a* in *man* to one like the *a* in *father.* The change affected words in which the vowel occurred before *f, sk, sp, st, ss, th,* and *n* followed by certain consonants. In parts of New England the same change took place, but in most other parts of this country the old sound was preserved. The flat *a* is regarded as the typical American pronunciation.[5]

Next to the retention of the flat *a*, the most noticeable difference between English and American pronunciation is the treatment of the *r*. Eastern New England and most of the South follow the English practice of dropping the speech sound of *r* when it occurs before another consonant (*lord = laud*) except before vowels (*carry, Tory*). The Southern dialect in most districts agrees with New England in this respect but tends to go even further and also weaken the *r* before vowels. In the middle states and the West the *r* is pronounced in all positions.

The American use of *gotten* in place of *got* as the past participle of *get* was the form used in England two centuries ago. We still use *mad* in the sense of *angry*, as Shakespeare and his contemporaries did, and we have kept the general significance of *sick* without restricting it to nausea. We still speak of *rare meat*, whereas the English say *underdone*. We have kept the word *fall* for the season; the English *autumn* is learned from books. The American *I guess* is as old as Chaucer and was still current in English speech in the 17th century.[6]

The rural speech of New England or of the Kentucky mountaineer shows hundreds of words, meanings, and pronunciations that are now obsolete in the standard speech of both England and this country. There can be no question that many older features of the language of England can be illustrated by survivals in this country.

There are current variations in pronunciation between British and American English. For one thing, many words which are not pronounced with the vowel of *meat* had, at the time of the earliest settlements in America, the quality of present-day English *mate*. In fact, Londoners were accustomed to hear both the *ee* and the *ay* sounds in such words as *meat, teach, sea, tea, lean,* and *beard.* There was much fluctuation in words which are generally spelled with *oo*— those of the *food, good,* and *flood* classes, respectively. It is within recent years that the pronunciation of many of these words has become standardized. All three of these words constitute one of Shakespeare's rhymes, and a half-century later Dryden rhymed *flood* with *mood* and *good.* Even today certain words of this class (*roof, room, root, hoof, coop, soot,* and so on) are pronounced variously in different parts of the United States.[7]

UNIFORMITY OF AMERICAN ENGLISH

Except for a few districts such as the region around Massachusetts Bay and the tidewater sections of Virginia, the most prominent factor in the populating of the United States was the constant mingling of settlers from one part with those from other parts. As the colonists moved north, south, and west, the speech patterns of the early settlers became the primary pattern in America.

Linguistically the circumstances under which the American population spread over the country had one important consequence: The English spoken in America shows a high degree of uniformity. Although there are sectional differences in New England, the South, the Middle West, and the Far West, the dialects are not so distinctive as those of England. In addition to a mobile population, in America there are such great communication facilities as the telephone, radio, and television.

The pronounced dialectal differences that mark the popular speech of different parts of England are unknown in the United States. In Great Britain, in addition to the standard English spoken by the educated, there are local peculiarities based on the earliest stages of the language. These old forms have been preserved in various ways so that the differences in the British Isles are quite well marked. Each county has its own local forms, and the speech of the North is very different from that of the South. For almost 200 years visitors from England and other countries have remarked that the mass of people in the United States speak better English than the mass of people in England do.

As a nation the people of the United States speak American English better than any other people speak their own language. There is little local variation, and in the matter of pronunciation there is general conformance to what is considered to be an educated standard. The American standard rests upon general use. This is not an imposed standard, and complete uniformity cannot be claimed for it. Different levels of usage, differences of pronunciation, and colloquial expressions must be recognized here as in other countries. But most of the features of American English are shared in common by all parts of the country.

SUGGESTIONS AND ACTIVITIES FOR THE COLLEGE STUDENT AND THE CLASSROOM TEACHER

1. What are the main dialects within the United States?[8] Do people living in different sections of the United States have difficulty in understanding each other? What problems do people living in the London area and in other sections of England have in understanding each other? (See appropriate notes in section at end of chapter for helpful references on certain problems.)

2. What differences are there between American and British usage?[9] What differences are there between Canadian English and American English?

3. What words differ in pronunciation (*cain't* for *can't*; *fuhther* for *further*) and in substitutes or synonyms (*faucet, tap*) in your local community?

4. What is the importance of studying place names?[10] How many places can you list which represent different national influences in the country?

5. If you have studied Latin, what Latin words and phrases can you identify in American English? How has usage changed meanings?

6. In the Latin words identified in American English, is the pronunciation Latin, English, or a combination of the two?[11]

7. Two historical dictionaries devoted to American English are *A Dictionary of American English* and *Dictionary of Americanisms*[12]. Use these or other such dictionaries to look up the following words to see when they were first recorded in American English and where they came from: *raccoon, skunk, moccasin, prairie, bureau, gopher, waffle, cockroach, mosquito.*

8. If you live in a town that retains some of the Old World flavor derived from its early foreign settlers, try to discover what words of foreign origin are generally known to the community. Has the pronunciation of these words changed over the years? What areas of life do they represent? Why are they used instead of American English words?

9. The early Puritan colonists were not lacking in learning, but they brought with them not only the standard forms of 17th-century English but dialectical forms as well. In the speech of the rural New Englander, some of these early forms of English may still be used. If you live in the New England states or have visited there,

can you identify some of these forms? Can you locate words or phrases in dictionaries of American English that were commonly used in England about the time the colonists came to America?

10. The speech of the Southern colonists retained more of the earlier features of the English mother country than did the speech of New England, as the Southerners had more frequent contact with England than the resourceful New Englanders did. Can you identify some of the pronunciations, as: *kettle, get, stead* as "kittle," "git," "stid"; *potato, window, fellow, tobacco,* with the ending pronounced as if spelled *-er; boil* and *hoist* as if spelled "bile" and "histe"?

11. The United States west of the seaboard was settled by people of diverse origins. The remarkable uniformity in American speech west of the Atlantic seaboard has penetrated other sections, resulting in a general standard of American speech. Can you note pronunciations, words, or expressions which differ from yours among children or adults? Record these on tape or paper for class discussion or analysis of differences.

12. At least 24 major American dialects have been listed (see Hans Kurath, *Linguistic Atlas of the United States*). The main American dialectal distinctions are in vocabulary. For example, there is an insect generally known as dragon-fly; in New England it is a devil's darning needle; in the Appalachians a snake feeder; in other parts of the South it is a snake doctor or mosquito hawk. Can you name other common things that have different names in sections of the United States, such as *sack*?

NOTES

1. H. L. Mencken, *The American Language*, 9th ed. (New York: Alfred A. Knopf, Inc., 1940).

2. Albert H. Marckwardt, *American English* (New York: Oxford University Press, Inc., 1958), pp. 14–16.

3. Noah Webster, *American Dictionary of the English Language* (S. Converse, 1828), Preface.

4. Thomas Pyles, *Words and Ways of American English* (New York: Random House, Inc., 1963), p. 61.

5. Albert A. Baugh, *A History of the English Language* 2nd ed., © 1957 (New York: Appleton-Century-Crofts, 1957), p. 434. By permission of Prentice-Hall, Inc., Englewood Cliffs, New Jersey.

6. Ibid., pp. 416–17.

7. Marckwardt, *American English,* pp. 11–12.

8. See W. Nelson Francis et al., *Structure of American English* (New York: Ronald Press Co., 1958).

9. See Simeon Potter, *Our Language* (New York: Penguin Press, 1965) and other sources.

10. See Robert L. Ramsay, *The Place Names of Franklin County, Missouri* (Columbia; University of Missouri Press, 1954); Edwin C. Gudde, *California Place Names* (Berkeley; University of California Press, 1969); F. G. Cassidy, *Dane County Place Names* (Madison: University of Wisconsin Press, 1968).

11. See Edwin Lee Johnson, *Latin Words of Common English* (Boston: D. C. Heath Co., 1971).

12. William A. Craigie and James R. Hulbert, eds., *A Dictionary of Americanisms on Historical Principles,* 4 vols. (Chicago: University of Chicago Press, 1938–44); Mitford M. Mathews, ed., *Dictionary of Americanisms on Historical Principles* (Chicago: University of Chicago Press, 1951).

Chapter 4

History of English Grammars

GRAMMAR BEGAN as a philosophical inquiry into the nature of language by such philosophers as Plato and Aristotle. Greek prestige in the ancient world resulted in Greek grammar becoming the model for the grammars of Latin and other languages. But Greek could not be a good model for these languages because the structure of every language is peculiar to itself. The Romans, who were not intellectual innovators, transferred the preexisting system of Greek grammar to Latin, with only minor adjustments. The Greek terminology was ultimately adapted from Latin to English and most other languages of Europe.

INFLUENCE OF GREEK AND LATIN ON ENGLISH

The inflectional devices of Latin and Greek were not applicable to English. Both Latin and Greek are rich in inflections. English has only two inflected active tenses, against six for Latin, but many more periphrastic verbal constructions than Latin had. But for two millennia, attitudes toward language have been colored by the assumption that the system of a language can be analyzed and prescribed by an intellectual tool that is inapplicable.[1]

The structure of every language is peculiar to itself, though there are similarities. The best description of the structure of a language or the grammar of a language derives from a careful examination of the language itself, not from an attempt to fit it into the pattern of another.

The etymology of the word "grammar" starts with the Greek *gamma*, a letter of the alphabet. The plural *grammata* develops in meaning through "letters," to "alphabet," to the "rudiments of writing," to the "rudiments of learning." From the adjective form *grammatike* comes the Latin *grammaticus*, a term that later became prevalent through Greek influence.[2]

Thus Western grammar began with the ancient Greeks. The idea that a word describing action is a verb (*rhema*) and one that performs an action is a noun (*onoma*) dates from Plato. Aristotle added conjunctions (*syndesmoi*), recognized that sentences have predicates, and was aware of three genders and of inflection (rhetoric, and so on). The Stoics attempted to separate linguistic study from philosophy and made important contributions to the discipline. In their writings are terms which are approximately equivalent to *noun, verb, conjunction, article, number, gender, case, voice, mood, and tense.*[3]

The contributions of the Greeks were indeed great, but for 20 centuries the work was carried on by slavish and unimaginative imitators who were incapable of developing the foundations of their predecessors. Especially in the less highly inflected languages like English and French, it was not recognized that the inflectional devices of Latin and Greek must have some counterpart in the structure of the modern language.

Up to about the 12th century, grammar was based on classical Latin. At that time the reintroduction of Greek philosophy had a tremendous impact on medieval thought. A grammatical example is this one from the 13th century:

> For a complete sentence, two things are necessary, namely a subject and a predicate. The subject is that which is being discussed; it is what determines the person of the verb. The

predicate is that which is expressed by the subject. Nouns were invented to provide subjects .... Verbs were invented to provide predicates.[4]

USES OF THE WORD "GRAMMAR"

In Western European history, grammar books were mainly grammars of Latin. Early English grammars were also based upon Latin grammars. These grammars informed the student how to use a foreign language correctly and warned him how to avoid using it incorrectly. They were mainly concerned with policing the language, not with understanding it. Accordingly, grammar is often used to mean correct or elegant speech, as against incorrect or crude speech.

The first edition of the *Encyclopaedia Britannica* (1768-71) defined "grammar as an art," or a method of furnishing "certain observations called rules, to which the methods of speaking used in this language may be reduced." This was followed by a definition of "grammar as a science" which "examines a certain standard by which different languages may be compared, and their several excellencies and defects pointed out." The latter definition referred to Universal Grammar.[5]

To many people a definition means little. As individuals hear or see the word "grammar," they often think of learning the parts of speech or diagramming sentences. To a few, grammar means studying or using "correct English." Modern linguists use the word to signify the way a language works, the way the semantic units (which may or may not be words) are handled so that connected discourse becomes possible.

A curious paradox exists in regard to grammar. On the one hand it is regarded as the dullest and driest of academic subjects. On the other hand it is a subject upon which people hold very dogmatic opinions which they defend with considerable emotion. Much of this prejudice stems from ignorance and confusion.

Actually, the word "grammar" is used to refer to three different things, and much of the emotional thinking about matters grammatical arises from confusion among these different meanings. The *first* thing meant by grammar is "the set of formal patterns in which the words of a language are arranged in order to convey larger meanings." The *second* meaning of grammar is "the branch of linguistic science which is concerned with the description, analysis, and formulation of formal language patterns." The *third* sense in which people use grammar is "linguistic etiquette." In this sense, the word is often coupled with a derogatory adjective. When we say that the expression "He ain't here" is "bad grammar," what we mean is that such an expression is bad linguistic manners in certain circles. Thus there are three meanings of grammar: a form of behavior, a field of study or a science, and a branch of etiquette.[6]

BEGINNINGS OF PRESCRIPTIVE GRAMMAR

To prescribe and to proscribe seem to have been coordinate aims of the grammarians of the 18th century. Many of the conventions now accepted were first stated in this early period. According to Albert Baugh, the distinction between *lay* and *lie* was specifically made then, as was the preference for *different from,* the differentiation of *between* and *among,* and the use of the comparative instead of the superlative where only two things are involved (the *larger,* not the *largest,* of two). . . . The proper case before the gerund was settled, as in *I don't like him doing that* or *his doing that.* Some grammarians were opposed to *his* in this construction, but Noah Webster held that this was "the genuine English idiom" and the only permissible form. This era is also responsible for the condemnation of the double negative. Robert Lowth, an 18th-century clergyman, made up a rule that has bound grammarians for generations: Two negatives in English destroy one another, or are equivalent to an affirmative.[7]

As English came to replace Latin as the language of scholarship, it was felt that it should be possible to control and dissect it, parse it and analyze it, as with Latin. The grammatical description that applied to Latin was superimposed on English. Regardless of the fact that English has its own forms and signals and ways of producing meaning, English grammars on the Latin model were written and taught in the schools.

THE 18TH-CENTURY GRAMMARIANS

Great interest in English grammar developed in the 18th century. Grammarians of this era attempted to formulate rules for deciding matters of syntax and usage. They also tried to improve the language by pointing out errors that were to be avoided. Rules were set forth without considering actual usage, and thus written and spoken English were separated more and more widely.

Baugh notes that the grammarians of the 18th century aimed to do three things: (1) to codify the principles of the language and reduce it to rule, (2) to settle disputed points and decide cases of divided usage, and (3) to point out common errors or what were supposed to be errors, and thus correct and improve the language.[8] These grammarians were not content to record facts however; they also pronounced judgment. Of two alternate forms of expression, one must be wrong; a choice must be made. So rules were laid down and illustrated with examples.

According to Baugh, during the decade beginning in 1760, a number of English grammars were printed. The compilers were equipped with a knowledge of the classical languages but with little knowledge of the structure of our language. Among the books printed was *The Rudiments of English Grammar* by Joseph Priestley, which insisted upon the importance of usage. This was followed by Robert Lowth's *Short Introduction to English Grammar,* which was printed in at least 22 editions during the 18th century. In 1784 Noah Webster published the second part of *A Grammatical Institute of the English Language,* which enjoyed much prestige in America and some circulation in England. These grammarians and many others were not content to record facts; they pronounced judgment as to correct and incorrect forms. They pointed out that the difficulty encountered in speaking and writing the English language was not in the language itself but in practice or usage.[9]

A more liberal view was expressed by Joseph Priestley in his *Rudiments of English Grammar,* a remarkably original book destined to be condemned by more dogmatic grammarians for nearly a century. Baugh quotes Priestley as stating that any group is

> . . . ill calculated to reform and fix a language. We need make no doubt but that the best forms of speech will, in time, establish themselves by their own superior excellence; and, in all controversies, it is better to wait the decisions of time, which are slow and sure, than to take those of synods which are often hasty and injudicious.[10]

Priestley tried consistently to record what he had observed, refraining from judgments of absolute right or wrong. His approach to language was broad and perceptive. He brought to grammar the scientific attitude of observation, critical evaluation, and generalization.

SCHOLARLY TRADITIONAL GRAMMAR

University scholars in Europe developed another grammatical tradition. Their reference grammars brought into play many divergent points of view and a variety of terminology. The school grammars had set forth a system of very definite answers; the scholarly works raised many unanswered questions. The two groups had different materials and unlike goals. The school grammarians had a narrow corpus of accepted sentences; the European scholarly grammarians had a large and growing body of literary excerpts. The general framework of scholarly grammar was organized around parts of speech and sentence elements.

Perhaps the greatest traditional grammarian was Otto Jespersen, who had a background in linguistics and introduced a considerable number of innovations, especially to the general framework of grammar. He based his treatment of syntax almost completely on meaning. In his *Essentials of English Grammar,* he classified the words of sentences into ranks: primary for the main sentence elements, secondary for their modifiers, and tertiary for modifiers of secondaries.[11] School textbooks were little influenced by Jespersen and others, but college textbooks made use of these works, especially Jespersen's.

For many years traditional grammar has been closely associated with prescription. Rules have been taught in the schools, not as descriptions of what actually occurs but as legislation establishing what should be said and written. Some of the rules have no apparent connection with actual usage; others are flatly in opposition to usage. The prescriptive viewpoint was widely held in American schools through the 19th century.

SUGGESTIONS AND ACTIVITIES FOR THE COLLEGE STUDENT AND THE CLASSROOM TEACHER

1. Thomas Pyles and John Algeo state that the English teacher has not clearly understood the difference between "teaching about" and "teaching how to" and thus has not separated them in the classroom. As a result, they feel, the classroom is a hodgepodge of material and method.[12] Which do you feel has greater emphasis in

the classroom—learning about the structure of our language, or how to use it? How can you teach what you believe to be useful and important?

2. Look into an old English grammar. How many types of declensions of nouns and adjectives can you find? What advantages can you list for the grammars of the 1970s over the older English versions? Over those of the early 1900s?

3. If you view English as a science, then the study of English calls for a systematic analysis of complex patterns that have grown up through the centuries by those using it, the kind of study the scientist devotes to his subject of investigation. Do you feel you are willing to accept the study of English as a science? What traditional rules, if any, are you unwilling to give up?

4. Can you find evidence to support the acceptance of "It's him" or "It's me" as good usage? Do you use these forms? Do you accept these forms from your students without question? If you do, how do you teach from a textbook that adheres to "It's I?"

5. What is the difference between formal and informal English? Where is each used? Bring in illustrations of each.[13]

6. Discuss grammar in its different senses—descriptive, prescriptive, historical, comparative.[14] Which of these are you willing to accept? Or do you prefer a combination?

7. There seem to be four concepts that apply to all languages—communication, language, word, and grammar. Aside from these, there are few terms that apply to all languages. Are common terms necessary for a universal grammar? Can you locate other terms that appear to apply to all languages?

8. During the era of "prescription" there was a notion that a rule of grammar is competent, in and of itself, to determine whether a usage is correct or incorrect. Is this idea accepted today? How can you explain the concept of good usage to your students? Is it necessary to quote a rule to support your explanation?

9. H. A. Gleason, Jr., advocates a change in the method of presentation of grammar which involves leading students to discover principles for themselves (inductive teaching) and making students critical about language and about understanding language.[15] What background information do you feel you need to teach grammar based on linguistic principles?

NOTES

1. Karl Dykema, "Where Our Grammar Came From," *College English,* 22 (April 1961): 457.
2. Ibid., pp. 455–56.
3. R. H. Robins, *Ancient and Medieval Grammatical Theory in Europe* (London: Longmans, 1951), pp. 20–35.
4. Dykema, "Where Our Grammar Came From," p. 463.
5. *Encyclopaedia Britannica* (Edinburgh, 1768–71), 1st ed., p. 728.
6. W. Nelson Francis, "Revolution in Grammar," *Quarterly Journal of Speech,* 40 (1954): 62.
7. Albert C. Baugh, *A History of the English Language* 2nd ed., © 1957 (New York: Appleton-Century-Crofts, 1957), pp. 335–36. By permission of Prentice-Hall, Inc., Englewood Cliffs, New Jersey.
8. Albert C. Baugh, *A History of the English Language* 2nd ed., © 1957 (New York: D. Appleton-Century Co., 1935), p. 333. By permission of Prentice-Hall, Inc., Englewood Cliffs, New Jersey.
9. Ibid., pp. 331, 333.
10. Joseph Priestley, *The Rudiments of English Grammar,* (London: R. Griffiths, 1761). Quoted in Baugh, *History of English Language,* pp. 326.
11. Otto Jespersen, *Essentials of English Grammar* (New York: Henry Holt, 1933).
12. Thomas Pyles and John Algeo, *English: An Introduction to Language* (New York: Harcourt, Brace & World, 1970).
13. See Porter G. Perrin, *Writer's Guide and Index to English* (Glenview, Ill.: Scott, Foresman & Co., 1968) for illustrations.
14. Ibid.
15. H. A. Gleason, Jr., *Linguistics and English Grammar.* New York: Holt, Rinehart & Winston, Inc., 1965.

PART TWO

Language and the Child

Chapter 5

Developmental Processes in the Child's Acquisition of Syntax

THE COMPLEX SYSTEM of speech sounds that is called language is the basic channel for human intellectual and social interaction. The birth cry signals the entrance of the human into a complicated social world in which language is the primary tool of communication.

At some time in the second six months of life most children say their first intelligible word. But the child's ability to pronounce sounds and to order them into words does not mean he has learned a language. This kind of imitating is readily taught to birds, and many other kinds of animals can be trained to respond to words or word combinations. During the first four years the child moves from mere vocalizing to creative, meaningful, purposeful language use. He produces new sentences never heard before, going well beyond imitation of those around him. Only when the child generates and comprehends sentences he has never heard before can it be said he has learned a language.

EARLY STAGES

Children throughout the world originally have the capacity for making all speech sounds. Some of these sounds are encouraged by the specific language heard, and others drop out because they are not part of the child's environment.

Psycholinguists view the child more as a "rule inducer" than as a learner of discrete items, from the early steps of word acquisition and naming (the base of all symbolization) to complex sentence development. Roger Brown and Ursula Bellugi have stated the hypothesis of the psycholinguists well:

> One must somehow account for the fact that, when children have heard a lot of speech, they start to talk, whereas, if apes hear the same noises, they do not talk. A "language generator" must be built into the brain and set to operate independent of any natural language. The character of possible language, or the set of possible grammars, must somehow be represented in the brain. In the broadest sense the language generator must contain the information-processing procedures which any human organism will use when exposed to some speech community. . . . The particular language, particular grammar and phonological system, are learned. When we talk of language acquisition, it is often in the sense of the child's internalization of the particular grammar to which he has been exposed.[1]

Babbling

The first stage in the acquisition of language is marked by the appearance of babbling. According to Otto Jespersen, babbling may start as early as the third week of life, but it usually starts around the seventh or eighth week.[2] The first babbling sounds probably have no referent but are merely muscular exercises. Babbling continues until the child starts to use words in a meaningful manner and persists more than a year after the child starts to talk.

A popular explanation of babbling is that it is a period in which the child refines those phonemes used by the adults with whom he associates and drops those phonemes that are unnecessary in the language he soon will speak, a phenomenon called *phonemic contraction*. This babbling is a period of practice during which the child perfects and completes his phonemic repertoire.

The earliest vocalizations of infants are vowel saturates; their cooing becomes interspersed with consonants by the age of five months. At six months the frequency and types of sounds uttered by deaf children become distinct from those of their age-mates.

In the first year of life the vowel speech sounds vocalized by infants are composed mainly of front and middle vowels. By 30 months, however, the distribution of percentages is similar to that for the English-speaking American adult. In studies of consonant articulation it is found that young infants use mainly voiceless, fricative, and plosive sounds; rarely do they use nasals, semivowels, and glides. Vowel sounds exceed consonants for the first year, after which there are more consonants than vowel types. At two and a half years almost all vowel sounds used by the adult and about two-thirds of the consonants used by the adult are present.[3]

How a child manages to make a match between his sounds and those of speakers in his environment is still an open and interesting question. All things considered, such as the infant's immature vocal and brain structures, it is an enormous feat for a baby to match his sound to that produced by another human being.

Vocabulary

The appearance of a baby's first word is a much recorded event. But there are differences in the definition of a word. It is difficult to state whether the child is actually using an utterance meaningfully—as a word—or the utterance is merely part of his normal babbling, with no definite referent intended. As noted above, most children say their first intelligible word some time in the second six months of life.

Between the ages of one and one and a half, a child speaks in single-word utterances. These early words do not have part-of-speech value to the child, although the adult calls them nouns, verbs, and adjectives, the contentives of lexical items of a vocabulary. Words take on value as a part of speech only when combined with other words, when their position or privilege of occurrence in a string of words identifies them as nouns, verbs, and adjectives. To the one-year-old child, all words are contentives and merely stand for and call to mind categories of similar events that have been abstracted cognitively from the flux of sensimotor experience: *shoe, spoon, car, drink, walk, go, pretty, dirty, all gone.* All words in the beginning vocabulary are on the same level of abstraction: They are labels for the developing categories of experience.[4]

SYNTAX IN CHILD LANGUAGE

Language does not come about by simple imitation. The child can repeat only that which is formed by rules he has already mastered. The child abstracts regularities or relations from the language he hears, which he then applies to building up language for himself as an apparatus of principles.

The child's one-word utterances, or holophrases, have semantically and syntactically a different range than the single-word utterances of older children and adults. First words tend to be nouns, verbs, and interjections. Their form is sometimes that of the repeated syllable, as in the child's modification of *flower* to *fa-fa*. This illustrates how children's comprehension precedes production.

Sometimes the syntactic devices the child has at his disposal are too primitive (at least from an adult perspective) to serve as vehicles for the expression for his ideas. In such cases it is interesting to observe how the child overcomes his syntactic deficiencies. In the stage of one-word utterances, however, the child does manage to express relations among several ideas. He may say: "Train. Train. Bump." "Cow. Moo." "Beep Beep. Trucks. Beep. Trucks. Trucks." There are pauses between words, often accompanied by falling intonation. Thus, speech is more than a collection of remarks—it is an act of communication wherein the speaker selects from his repertoire whatever symbols and syntactic structures seem to him to be adequate and appropriate.

Patricia Carlson and Moshe Anisfeld report that at 29 months a boy they were studying had begun to use "because" in his sentences, as in "I can't clap because I'm a boy." Asking for a forbidden jar which was out of reach, the boy said, "I need a honey girl. Because I *need* it." At this age he could deliberately manipulate segmental phonemes in some ways, as in substituting one for another in songs. To the tune of "The Bear Went over the Mountain," he sang "Da de de doder da doundin"; to the tune of "I've Been Working on the Railroad," he sang "I pin purkin' on a pail poad." Soon afterwards he was able to control rhymes by giving a rhyming word on command or in a song which required it.[5]

The rapid development of language is also evident in that a child who is not able to produce initial *s* plus consonant clusters may begin to produce them all at approximately the same time (thus distinguishing for the first time between *cool* and *school,* for example), and characteristically will do this in just the right words. This indicates that the correct phonemic representation of these words was present to the mind at the stage where it did not appear in speech.

One cannot assume that a child's grammar is a form of the adult's. When a child's remarks are understood by an adult whose awareness of structure is explicit, it is possible for that adult to assign an immediate constituent analysis to those remarks. Hazel Francis, in analyzing the utterances of her son from the ages of two years seven months to two years ten months, found that many utterances could be matched with sentences having immediate constituents of noun phrase and verb phrase, where these in turn contained further elements. In strings of sentence patterns (noun phrase + *be* + adjective or further noun phrase), the main verb *be* was omitted from the verb phrase, although in other remarks it was included. The development of the auxiliary was much more complicated, as noted in these grammatical errors and omissions: "A police car go up there." "He be sick." "Mine gone up there." "I going on a horse."[6]

Research seems to indicate that young children classify words into parts of speech according to the adult model before they begin to use these words in parts of speech other than those in which they heard them. A noise which was "loud" was later used in an utterance as "a louding plane" by Francis' son. The -*ing* form was applied in an utterance at bath time, "Don't wash that poor little sore, because it's still soring."

The child between the ages of one and a half and two years appears to have a repertoire of noun phrase, verb, prepositional phrase, adjective, and adverb, based on operational categories. Francis's child was able to arrange these in sentence form according to his perceptions of a situation and his acceptance of the simple order used in the fragments of adult speech that he could understand. This was a development from the two-word pivot type of remark described by W. R. Miller and S. M. Erwin and by M. D. S. Braine,[7] but the remarks by Francis' son had the same characteristics in constituent pivot-open patterning. Examples are:

Noun phrase–Verb:	Verb–Noun phrase:
adverb	participle
adjective	prepositional phrase
prepositional phrase	adverb

When put together these produced a fragmentary hierarchical system.[8] This pivot-open patterning is, of course, reminiscent of the complex organization of children's collections described by L. S. Vygotsky.[9]

In the natural situation of the child with his family, the best evidence that the child possesses construction rules is the occurrence of systematic errors, according to Roger Brown and Colin Fraser. So long as a child speaks correctly, he may be saying only what he has heard. In general, it is not possible to know what the total input has been or how to eliminate the possibility of an exact model for each sentence that is uttered. When a young child says, "I digged in the yard" or "I saw some sheeps" or "Johnny hurt hisself," however, it is unlikely that he is imitating. Furthermore, his mistake is not a random one. Many verbs ending in voiced consonants form the simple past with -*d*, and many nouns ending in voiceless consonants form the plural with -*s*. The sets of forms *me, my, myself* and *you, your, yourself* strongly suggest *he, his, hisself*. As it happens, actual English usage breaks with these simple regularities, and in the child's examples, *dug, sheep,* and *himself* would be preferred.[10]

By smoothing the language into a simpler system than it is, the child reveals his tendency to induce rules. The child systematizes his language in his early utterances, and irregularities inherent in the adult language usually appear later. For example, internal borrowing or *analogy* is the kind of change employed when a child says *foots* instead of *feet, oxes* instead of *oxen, sticked* instead of *stuck,* or *breaked* instead of *broke*. Through such "errors" the child is revealing a knowledge of one of the rules of forming plurals: He is simply not aware of all the exceptions. If instead the child had said "feet," one could not be certain that the plural rule was understood. The child could actually know the plural as an irregular form, or he could just be imitating an adult.

The child has heard and learned many "regular" formations—plural formations such as *root-roots, hat-hats, book-books, map-maps* and past formations like *kick-kicked, rake-raked,* in the hundreds. He has made his new formation of a plural for *foot* or *ox* by abstracting the "regular" ending -*s* or -*es* and adding it to *foot* or *ox*. Likewise, he has added the "regular" past ending -*ed* to *break* on the analogy of other past tenses like *kicked, raked*. Thus the child is making what may be termed analogical new formations.

Such observations of "errors" have been helpful in studying grammatical development. "Errors" such as these occur infrequently in the child's speech, so the amount of speech that has to be examined in order to gain a thorough knowledge of the child's morphological rules is very large.

In an effort to avoid this problem, James Berko devised a method for testing a child's knowledge of grammatical rules involved in forming plurals, past tenses, diminutives, derived adjectives, third-person singulars, possessives, comparatives and superlatives, progressive and derived compounds, and compounded or derived words. Pictures were presented, and the child was told something about the picture and given a sentence to complete. In testing plurals the child was shown a picture of a birdlike object and then a picture of two of them. He was told: "This is a wug. Now there is another one. There are two of them. There are two _____". Variants of the plural morpheme were tested by using different nonsense names. Thus *wug* should elicit -*z,* while *tass* should elicit *ez.* The subjects included children four to seven years and adults. Subjects were able to form plurals, verb forms, and possessives with a relatively high degree of skill but were not so successful in inflecting adjectives, deriving and compounding new words, or analyzing compound words.[11]

Morphology (patterns of word formation) is relatively unimportant in English, while syntax (patterns of formation of sentences and phrases from words) is quite important. An English-speaking child can say "five boy" instead of "five boys" and still be understood; however, ambiguity as to meaning would result if he says "boys five."

Roger Brown, Courtney Cazden, and Ursula Bellugi documented striking similarities in sequence of acquisition, regardless of large differences in the rate of grammatical acquisition. They also indicated that the young children studied did not combine words randomly; their errors were those of omission and overgeneralization. In both instances, the children were thought to be in the process of developing patterns of their own instead of imitating adult patterns.[12]

Cazden studied the errors in noun and verb inflections in the speech of three Cambridge children, studied longitudinally by Roger Brown, and twelve black children in a Roxbury, Massachusetts day care center: "The overgeneralizations made by the two groups (Cambridge and Roxbury) are strikingly similar in kind, though not of course in absolute numbers. The Roxbury children not only make the same kind of errors; they even make them with some of the identical words. While we cannot assume that similar or even identical forms necessarily have the same status in different language systems, the similarities across these 14 children, despite differences in their home dialect, are too numerous to be dismissed . . .

To the extent that analogical errors indicate children's syntactic rules, these data suggest that dialect differences do not make much difference at these early stages. It seems likely that those parts of the structure of English which children learn first are the same across dialects, and it seems even more likely that the strategies or processes by which children learn that structure are also the same."[13]

Although many research workers expected to find pervasive differences in grammatical skills as a function of social class to substantiate further the linguistic deficiency hypotheses, the differences that emerge are limited. There is evidence to support the position that children in different dialect communities have identical grammars up to a point (though their parents do not). These might be rules which in fact disappear in later stages of development.

GRAMMATICAL SYSTEMS FOR ENCODING AND DECODING

Some research shows that an individual has two grammatical systems, one for encoding and another for decoding, or an active and passive grammatical system. The assumption underlying this view is that the speaker's behavior should be modeled by one sort of system and the hearer's by another. There appears to be no precise characterization for a "grammar for the encoder" or a "grammar for the decoder" that is not convertible, by a notational change, into the other. For the adult, then, a single grammar can normally account for almost all of both systems. The adult can interchange his encoding and decoding systems at will.

However, a child in the beginning stages of learning his language must understand a grammatical pattern before he can produce it. This understanding may be almost instantaneous, or it may develop gradually. This learning stage indicates the interdependence of the encoding and decoding systems; it appears that one is derived from the other. The grammar that represents the speaker's competence is, of course, involved in both his speaking and his interpretation of speech, and there seems to be no reason to assume that there are two different underlying systems, one involved in speaking, one in understanding.

Sentences

Before the child utters his first two-word sentence there is a long period during which he passively understands sentences, although he does not use them. The child's first true sentence is a shortened, telegraphic version of adult speech. These sentences usually contain only content words and require the listener to add the function words he considers necessary on the basis of his knowledge of the child and the situation. The utterance *I go* could mean *I am going* or *I want to go,* depending on whether the child is getting ready to go some place with his parents or is watching them go some place without him.

Imitation and Reduction

The transcribed dialogue of two young children designated by Roger Brown and Ursula Bellugi as "Adam" and "Eve" offers interesting comparisons with adult speech. The mother's speech to her child differs from the speech that adults use to one another. Her sentences are short, simple, and often repetitive. Thus the child's introduction to English comes in the form of a simplified, repetitive, and idealized dialect.

A section from "Adam's" first recording is given in Table 1. Notice that the imitations preserve the word order of the model sentences. Words are often missing, but the preservation of order suggests that the model sentence is processed by the child as a total construction rather than as a list of words. This kind of reduction was very common in the speech of the two children studied.

TABLE 1
Section from "Adam's" First Recording

Adam	Mother
See truck, Mommy	
See truck.	
	Did you see the truck?
No I see truck.	
	No, you didn't see it?
	There goes one.
There go one.	
	Yes, there goes one.
See a truck.	
See truck, Mommy.	
See truck.	
Truck.	
Put truck, Mommy.	
	Put the truck where?
Put truck window.	
	I think that one's too large
	to go in the window.

Imitation with Expansion

Adult expansion of child speech is quite common. The words spoken by the mother preserve the order of the words in the child's sentences. Words and inflections are added, but they are fitted in—before, after, and between the words the child uses. In Table 2, also based on Brown and Bellugi's study, notice the character of the forms added by the mother to the child's utterances. They include the auxiliaries *is* and *will;* the prepositions *in, on, to,* and *up;* the verb forms *is, have, had,* and *having;* the articles *a* and *the;* and the pronouns *he, her,* and *it.*

TABLE 2
Expansions of Child Speech Produced by Mothers

Child	Mother
Babby highchair	Baby is in the highchair
Mommy eggnog	Mommy had her eggnog
Eve lunch	Eve is having lunch
Mommy sandwich	Mommy'll have a sandwich
Sat wall	He sat on the wall
Throw Daddy	Throw it to Daddy
Pick glove	Pick the glove up

Source: Roger Brown and Ursula Bellugi, "Three Processes in the Child's Acquisition of Syntax," *Harvard Educational Review,* 34 (1964): 144.

In Table 2 the first set of utterances produced by the child are all of the same grammatical type; all four consist of a proper noun followed by a common noun, but each is expanded in different ways. The form of the verb added changes: in the first case it is the simple present tense; in the second, the simple past; in the third, the present progressive; in the last, the simple future. Each of the second set of utterances consists of a verb followed by a noun. The expansions are all grammatical but quite unlike, especially with regard to the preposition supplied.[14]

There appears to be little evidence that expansions are necessary for learning either grammar or sentence construction. Some parents and nursery school teachers do expand, and children do learn from it. Most expansions are responsive not only to the child's words but also to the circumstances attending their utterance. By adding something to the words the child has just produced, one confirms his response insofar as it is appropriate. Expansions add meaning at a moment when the child is most likely to be attending to the cues that can teach that meaning.

In fact, when the child is not talking with adults he reflects in his speech his own mode of operating in the world, although he may at times repeat well-rehearsed items of songs, rhymes, and snatches of adult language. Exposure to more adult speech presents him with the opportunity of acquiring a little more than he expects or understands, and if the heard remark refers to ongoing, meaningful activity then the little extra may be attended to, considered, and eventually tried out to see what happens. Slowly the child adds to his repertoire, not using simply the syntax of language but what might be called the syntax of experience of the relations between his functioning brain and body and the rest of the world.

Studies of early child language show that the child's speech is intimately linked to the immediate behavioral setting. The conversations are tagged on to contemporaneous objects and events. These studies show no speech of the sort that Leonard Bloomfield called "displaced," that is, speech about other times and other places.[15] The conversations were very much in the here and now.

Imitation and Construction

So long as a child speaks as correctly as the adults he hears, there is no way to tell whether he is simply repeating what he has heard or whether he is actually constructing. However, when he says something like "I digged a hole" he can be assumed to be constructing, because it is unlikely that he would have heard *digged* from anyone.

Acceptance of the concept that a child's grammar is simply an abbreviated form of adult grammar supports the finding that imitated sentences become more like the original ones (those spoken by the adult) with increasing age. There is also a tendency for the same morphemes to be omitted by different children but for the word order to be preserved—indicators of the strength of syntax in English. The fact that the child's first sentences preserve the word order of their models partially accounts for the ability of an adult to "understand" these sentences and to feel that he is in communication with the child.

As the child repeats the sentences of the adult and makes utterances of his own, he is likely to retain the "open" classes of words as nouns, verbs, and adjectives. Thus the words used have semantic content and are called "contentives." This telegraphic transformation of English generally communicates very well. It does so because it retains the high-information words that carry meaning. Then, too, it appears the child retains the words on which the heavier stresses fall. In a construction such as *Push car* programmed as a single utterance, the primary stress falls on *car*, thus unifying the two words. With sentences such as *Want baby, Want horsie, It horsie*, it is quite possible that the sentence *It baby* would be used in the future.

USE OF PIVOTS IN WORD COMBINATIONS

The use of syntax begins somewhere between 18 months and two years. Several separate psycholinguistic studies have announced similar findings that a set of rather abstract words called "pivots" appears in children's first word combinations, usually in the initial position, with the contentive or open-class word following. These pivots include the articles, *a* and *the;* quantity words such as *some, all, no, more;* designative words such as *here, there, this, that, it;* and position words in combination with verbs, such as *fall down, stand up, put on, take off.* The pivot plus open-class combination has become recognized as a child's first grammatical structure. It allows such typical word combinations as *a doggie, the car, more cookie, no milk, there shoe, here baby, that truck, sit down, turn off.* Occasionally two open-class words are combined. Two nouns make an immature possessive, *Daddy hat;* an adjective and a noun make an immature noun phrase, *big car;* a verb and noun make a short verb phrase, *see horse, turn wheel, read book.* While these are not subject-predicate sentences by adult grammatical standards, they are complete sentences in child grammar. They express an entire, unified bit of information, and the child seems to consider them complete statements.[16]

A step in syntactic development is the recognition of the noun phrase as an independent grammatical unit. There is a cohesiveness about the noun and its modifiers that allows them to be moved about in a string of words, preserving their grammatical integrity. The pivot combinations are now expanded to include noun modifiers in their proper sequence. *That doggie* becomes *that a doggie* or *that a big doggie; car dirty* becomes *the car dirty* or *Daddy car dirty; read book* becomes *read a book* or *read more book.* Such constructions are usually developed before the age of three. The next step in grammatical structure is the addition of the subject to form a subject-predicate, actor-action sentence. Laura Lee identifies typical three-year-old sentences as: designative (*There's a car, It is a house, That's a doggie*); predicative (*The light is on, The dress is pretty, Spot is a good dog*); actor-action (*The boy sit down, Me put on a hat, The doggie run away*).[17]

EXPANDING KERNEL SENTENCES

Several researchers indicate that the child's language development does not stop with the formation of basic subject-predicate sentences.[18] The three-year-old child embarks upon another stage of language growth. His basic kernel sentences are transformed into other types through the use of negatives, interrogatives, passives, and so on. He learns to conjoin two sentences, to subordinate some sentences to others, or to include one sentence within another by means of infinitives, participles, and gerunds. He learns the elaborate English verb tenses and modifies the "*is* of identity" and the "*is* of predication" (see below) from *it is* into *it was, it should be, it could have been.*

Always as the substrate of any transformational structure, however, lies the kernel sentence, a basic linguistic unit, a bit of verbal information all children learn between the ages of two and three. All adult sentences can be reduced from their transformational complexity into one or more of three underlying kernel sentence types. The classification of developmental sentence types described below closely parallels the kinds of sentences that Alfred Korzybski describes as "*is* of identity" (*This is a knife*), "*is* of predication" (*The knife is sharp*), and "subject-predicate" (*The knife cuts*).[19]

Types of Statements

Three distinct types of statements have been described by Lee.[20] With considerable uniformity, normally developing children seem to have three different kinds of things to say, three varieties of verbal observations. The first of these is "designative construction," which merely points out and names an item of attention: *Here a horsie, That a big car, It a funny hat.* The designative words *here, there, this, that,* and *it,* which were pivot words in an earlier stage, seem now to serve as verbal replacements for a pointing gesture, accompanied by the naming of objects. Designative statements are common in the speech of children two and a half years old.

The second type of statement, called the "predicative construction," includes a noun phrase followed by an adjective, prepositional phrase, or another noun, as: *The milk all gone, The car in garage, Billy a good boy.* These constructions are noun phrase expansions of their earlier two-word counterparts.

The third type of statement contains a verb but is a verb phrase only; the subject is missing. The child who says *Have a cookie* is not inviting you to take one; rather, he is announcing that he himself has a cookie. He accompanies his play with predicates describing his own activities: *See a big car, Put it here.* These constructions are expansions of the two-word, verb-object combinations.

STYLES OF COMMUNICATION

Separate conversations may deal with the very same objects and be oriented toward precisely the same task but nevertheless differ markedly. This is clearly shown in a systematic analysis of maternal teaching styles by R. D. Hess and V. C. Shipman.[21] Black mothers and children, of both low and middle classes, were brought to the laboratory at the University of Chicago Early Education Research Center. Each mother was to teach the same content to her child. The wide range of individual differences in linguistic and interactional styles can be illustrated by excerpts from recordings of these transactions. The task of the mother was to teach the child how to group or sort a small number of toys. To be effective, the mothers had to be able to communicate specific meanings clearly and precisely, as in the following example:

> *First Mother:* All right, Susan, this board is the place where we put the little toys; first of all you're supposed to learn how to place them according to color. Can you do that? The things that are all the same color you put in one section; in the other section you put another group of colors, and in the third section you put the last group of colors. Can you do that? Or would you like to see me do it first?
> *Child:* I want to do it.
> *Second Mother* (introducing the same task): Now I'll take them all off the board; now you put them all back on the board. What are these?

Child: A truck.
Second Mother: All right, just put them right here; put the other one right here; all right put the other one there.[22]

The first mother (middle class) introduced the particular toys with the abstract definite article plus noun groups of words ("the toys," "the things") while the second mother (lower class) made sole use of purely deictic (or demonstrative) words ("them," "these"). In the first case references are made to subsets of objects ("things that are the same color," "another group of colors," "the last group of colors"), which also involve abstract conceptual strategies. The second mother's reference to subsets as "the other" and "the other one" is devoid of such strategies.

Ragnar Rommetveit points out that the board in this experiment is also dealt with in distinctively different ways. In the first conversation there is an abstract linguistic elaboration of its spatial functional properties ("this board," "the place where we put the little toys," "one section," "the other section," "the third section"). The second mother, on the other hand, sticks very closely to what is perceptually given ("the board," "right here," "there"). Then note how the first mother presupposes (and exploits) the child's capacity to tag "pro words" such as "do" and "that" onto cognitions introduced by previous speech. The first "do that" refers to "place them according to color." When "do that" is said the second time, this cognition has been further elaborated by reference to three sections of the board and three color groups. The "do it" in the child's "I want to do it" is thus actually the sixth link in an anaphoral deictic chain, initiated by the phrase "place them according to color."[23] ("Them" was already at the very beginning partly emancipated from unique perceptual characteristics by the mother's identifying phrases "the little toys" and "the things.")

Such differences in conversation styles were frequently found in this study between upper-middle-class (as illustrated by the first mother) and culturally deprived (the second mother) homes. Hess and Shipman maintained that "the meaning of deprivation is a deprivation of meaning."[24]

Further evidence of different conversation styles was noted in the Hess and Shipman study in the praise and encouragement of successful mothers and the criticism and coercive control of others to motivate their children. When the child made a mistake, some mothers simply said, "That's not right," "Pay attention now and get it right," or "No, that's not what I showed you!" leaving him in the dark as to what to do next. In contrast other mothers would point to the erroneously placed block and the other blocks and say, "No, see, this block has an O on it and these have X's. You don't want to mix up the O's and the X's, so you have to put this block where there are some other blocks that have O on them, too." or "No, . . . That's a big one. Remember we're going to keep the big ones separate from the little ones." Children of mothers who explained the task were more successful in completing it than were children whose mothers could not transmit information specifically enough to teach the child what to do.

Teachers and other adults working with young children can discover ways of helping children accomplish goals by giving specific explanations and encouraging any attempt to reach a goal or solve a problem.

SUGGESTIONS AND ACTIVITIES FOR THE COLLEGE STUDENT AND THE CLASSROOM TEACHER

1. Tape a young child's (one and a half to five years of age) spontaneous speech while he is playing with a toy or any activity in which there is little or no adult speech. If you are a college student, play the tape for your classmates. Analyze the tape for vocabulary extent, repetitions, parts of speech, made-up words, and unidentifiable words.

2. Make up some model sentences for a two- or three-year-old and use them with a child (see Tables 1 and 2 as guides). Tape-record your model sentences and the child's responses. Check your recording to notice (1) whether the imitations preserve the word order of the model sentences, (2) what words were omitted, (3) whether the words you stressed were in the child's imitation, and (4) whether the child's responses increased in length with increase in model utterance.

3. The young child is able to understand and construct sentences he has never heard. How do linguists explain this ability?

4. Children who hear people talking start to talk at about or shortly after the first year. Apes who hear speech do not talk. Can you account for the young child's ability to speak without being taught the word formations?

5. How does the child acquire language? Does the child have the "innate" capacity to learn language, as the theories of Noam Chomsky and Eric Lenneberg would suggest?[25]

6. All words in the beginning vocabulary stand for and call to mind events. Do these words have part-of-speech value, or do they just stand for events?

7. Since a child must understand a grammatical pattern before he can produce it, would it add to your information in studying the young child's language to listen for and record such "errors" as *foots* for *feet*? Are "errors" more common than "normal" speech?

8. Secure or try to develop some experimental materials such as toys or blocks which can be grouped according to color, size, or letter. Try out your materials with preschoolers, using various methods:

   a. Giving little explanation or help.
   b. Pointing out errors.
   c. Supportive comments and helpful suggestions.

   Enlist the help of three of your classmates and use at least three preschoolers with cooperative parents, if possible. Tape-record your experiment.

9. Are verbs more difficult for young children to learn than nouns? V. P. John found that lower-class black preschoolers experience much more difficulty with action (verbs) than with object (noun) items. He states that it takes more one-to-one verbal interaction (with its corrective feedback) between a child and a more mature speaker of a language to learn a label for an action than for an object.[26] Is this related to the quality or the quantity of language heard? What effect does inadequate linguistic labels have on the verbal interactions in which the child participates with an older sibling or an adult?

10. What do linguists recognize as the child's first grammatical structure? Select a group of pivot words such as those used in combination with verbs—take off, put down. How many combinations can you make? How do repeated uses of the same word in other combinations expand and intensify meanings for the child?

NOTES

1. Roger Brown and Ursula Bellugi, "Three Processes in the Child's Acquisition of Syntax," *Harvard Educational Review,* 34 (1964): 133. Copyright © 1964 by President and Fellows of Harvard College.

2. Otto Jespersen, *Language: Its Nature, Development, and Origin* (London: Allen & Unwin, 1922).

3. Freda G. Rebelsky et al., "Language Development—The First Four Years," in *Infancy and Early Childhood,* ed. Yvonne Brackbill (New York: Free Press, 1967), p. 300.

4. Laura L. Lee, "The Relevance of General Semantics to the Development of Sentence Structure in Children's Language," in *Communication: General Semantics Perspectives,* ed. Lee Thayer (New York: Spartan Books, 1970), p. 118.

5. Patricia Carlson and Moshe Anisfeld, "Some Observations on the Linguistic Competence of a Two-Year-Old Child," *Child Development,* 40 (1969): 572, 574. By permission of the Society for Research in Child Development.

6. Hazel Francis, "Structure in the Speech of a 2½-Year-Old," *British Journal of Educational Psychology,* 39 (1969): 293. By permission of Scottish Academic Press, Limited.

7. W. R. Miller and S. M. Ervin, "The Development of Grammar in Child Language," *Child Development Monographs,* 39 (1964): 9–34; M. D. S. Braine, "The Ontogeny of English Phrase Structure: The First Phrase," *Language,* 39 (1963): 1–13.

8. Francis, "Structure in Speech of 2½-Year-Old," p. 294.

9. L. S. Vygotsky, *Thought and Language* (New York: John Wiley & Sons, Inc., 1962).

10. Roger Brown and Colin Fraser, "The Acquisition of Syntax," In Ursula Bellugi and Roger Brown (eds.) *The Acquisition of Language. Monographs of the Society for Research in Child Development,* 39 (1964): 43-49 (Chicago: University of Chicago Press, 1964) © 1964 by The University of Chicago.

11. J. Berko, "The Child's Learning of English Morphology," *Word,* 14 (1958): 150–77.

12. Roger W. Brown, Courtney B. Cazden, and Ursula Bellugi, "The Child's Grammar from 1 to 111," in *Minnesota Symposium on Child Psychology,* vol. II, ed. J. P. Hill, 5 vols. (Minneapolis: University of Minnesota Press, 1969). Copyright © 1969 by the University of Minnesota.

13. Courtney B. Cazden, *Child Language and Education* (New York: Holt, Rinehart and Winston, 1972), p. 48.

14. Brown and Bellugi, "Child's Acquisition of Syntax," pp. 133–51.

15. Leonard Bloomfield, *Language* (New York: Henry Holt & Co., 1933).

16. Braine, "Ontogeny of English Phrase Structure"; Brown & Fraser, "Acquisition of Syntax"; Miller and Ervin, "Grammar in Child Language."

17. Lee, "Relevance of General Semantics," pp. 119–20.

18. Ibid., pp. 120–21; Noam Chomsky, *Syntactic Structures* (The Hague, Netherlands: Mouton, 1957).

19. Alfred Korzybski, *Science and Sanity: An Introduction to Non-Aristotelian Systems and General Semantics,* 4th ed. (Lakeville, Conn.: International Non-Aristotelian Library Publishing Co., 1958), p. 371.

20. Lee, "Relevance of General Semantics," p. 119.

21. R. D. Hess and V. C. Shipman, "Early Experience and the Socialization of Cognitive Modes in Children," *Child Development,* 36 (1966): 869–86. By permission of the Society for Research in Child Development.

22. Ibid, p. 881.

23. Ragnar Rommetveit, *Words, Meanings, and Messages* (New York: Academic Press, 1968), p. 195.

24. Hess and Shipman, "Early Experience and Cognitive Modes," p. 885.

25. Noam Chomsky, *Aspects of the Theory of Language.* (Cambridge, Mass.: The M.I.T. Press, 1965); Eric Lenneberg, *The Biological Bases of Language* (New York: John Wiley & Sons, Inc., 1967).

26. V. P. John, "The Intellectual Development of Slum Children: Some Preliminary Findings," *American Journal of Orthopsychiatry,* 33 (1963): 813–22.

Chapter 6

Language Development and the School Child

BY THE TIME the child reaches school age he has already learned to use the sound system, grammar, and vocabulary of the home and neighborhood. He employs all the common sentence patterns identified as basic to the English language.

The child entering the first grade can make sentences, most of them quite new and created on the spot to meet the needs of the moment. He is able to understand English—that is, to listen to a sentence and figure out its structure and, hence, its meaning. This does not hold true for *any* English sentence; the child's knowledge of the language does have limits. But even the most poorly endowed child has an incredibly wide variety of patterns he can and does use. Most children frequently put together new patterns just as adults do. The six-year-old child certainly knows a great deal of the system of the language.

Although the child is able to use basic sentence patterns, he cannot explain how or why he uses these patterns. He cannot even tell how a certain sentence means what it does. But he does know what it means, and he can make sentences to mean what he wants to say some, if not all, of the time. His major deficiency is not in knowledge of the language system but in his ability to talk about it. Knowledge of grammar rules and how they describe his language patterns will develop as needed.

PRESCHOOL AND SCHOOL LEARNING

Language acquisition is a current interest of psycholinguists. Many tape recordings have been made of children in the process of language learning, and the child's spontaneous utterances have been analyzed over a period of years.

It is universal that all children learn language merely by being placed in the environment of the language, and they do not need any special training or conditioning whatever to achieve this.[1] All children also appear to learn language in about the same length of time, from four to six years. And all have rules by which they produce their language at each stage of the acquisition process, regardless of the particular language or form of language they are acquiring.[2]

A grammar can be written for a particular child's language at any stage of his development. From the linguistic data obtained, one can determine the precise grammatical rules under which he is operating and can predict the next rules that he will generate.

Early language acquisition involves very complex patterns of interrelated part processes. The acquisition of the inflectional system seems to involve rule learning of some kind, but it is also related to acquisition of word meanings as in contrasts like *dogs bark / dog barks.*

Children as young as four and a half to five years usually have mastered paired words such as *you are, are you.* The cohesion of groups of words such as *you are, I do, It is* may stem from the sheer articulatory chunking of the two words in adult speech, although in rapid speech the sound of the second word may be obscured, as in *You're, I'd, It's.* This also holds true of segments like *don't* and *can't* which constitute very important and semantically unequivocal constituents of the adult's messages to the young child, frequently accompanied by nonlinguistic signs of prohibition.[3]

The native language is learned in stages. According to Martin Joos, each stage is completed while the next is in progress. The first stage is learning the entire pronunciation system, which is completed before the child enters school. The second stage is learning the grammatical system; this begins about a year later than the first stage began and is completed at about eight years of age. In the third stage, which begins when the first stage is ending, the meanings of the words currently known begin to be organized into semantic systems of similarity, contrast, and hierarchy. This process continues uninterruptedly for a good many years.[4]

By age six the child already has as firm a grasp as he ever will have of the structure of his language. Slips like *tooken* for *taken* or *put down it* for *put it down* are simply part of the long process of trial and error by which the child has been learning his native language ever since he was one or two years old. These are analogical substitutions which will probably be ironed out in a year or so, whether he has formal instruction in grammar or not. Everyone makes similar analogical formations from time to time, which may be termed "slips of the tongue."

LINGUISTS AND EDUCATORS

Recently there has been greater contact between linguists and psychologists concerning language and language learning, cognition, and speech. Some of this contact has been related to the language curriculum.

The most significant research at present is on language learning in children. For some years linguists and educators have held opposing views. When linguists maintain that a child of six coming to school for the first time knows his language, they mean, of course, the basic structures of the language. Educators and linguists agree that children are able to put together sentences accurately and effectively. Linguists feel that while the vocabulary of school children is much larger than has been estimated, vocabulary is a more or less incidental aspect of language, coming and going with the needs of the speaker.

The process of learning a language is far more complex than early studies indicated. Educators assumed a simple notion of language; linguists underestimated the complexity of the learning process; psychologists limited research studies. Currently there are a number of research centers using carefully controlled observation and ingenious experimentation to make adequate appraisals of the child's actual command of language and the processes by which it is built up. Some of these studies, such as those by Brown and Bellugi, were cited in Chapter 5.

All speakers of a language above the age of five or six know how to use its complex forms of organization with considerable skill; in this sense of the word, they are thoroughly familiar with its grammar. They have mastered the sound system of their language, and they can put words together to express meanings. By three years of age some children are so advanced in the sentence construction process that they are able to produce all of the major varieties of English simple sentences, up to a length of 10 or 11 words.

The child of six uses every part of speech and every form of sentence. From the first few months of his life the child has had constant practice in the use of language. His need to communicate has been so great that he has acquired patterns which his environment has furnished without regard to their correctness in the eyes of later teachers. In fact, the child's spoken language has reached 90 percent of its mature level, when judged on the basis of sentence structure, before the child knows that grammar exists.

NOUN PLURAL DEVELOPMENT: AN EXAMPLE

One aspect of language development which has been studied quite extensively is the ability of children at various age levels to form plurals. James Berko developed a series of tests to investigate the child's internalization of a variety of morphological rules. Both real and nonsense words were used with cartoonlike drawings to illustrate one or more than one figure. Berko found that preschool and first-grade children were generally able to form plurals for new words requiring -s and -z, but were frequently unable to form plurals for new words requiring -ez. He used only one real word *(glass)*, plus four nonsense words *(wug, lun, tor,* and *cra)* which regularly form the plural with -z and four nonsense words *(tass, gutch, kazh,* and *nizz)* which regularly form the plural with -ez. Further details of this study are given in Chapter 5.[5]

Michael Graves and Stephen Koziol expanded earlier studies by setting up six types of plural-formation patterns for children in the first, second, and third grades. Series of 13 real words and 21 nonsense words were presented, randomly ordered. They concluded that certain patterns of plural formation are mastered before others. Children in the first grade have largely mastered the pluralization rules for words which regularly take an -s or -z allomorph. Many children do not gain mastery over the -ez allomorph until some point in the third grade.[6]

For mastery of the words in the patterns presented in the Graves and Koziol study, children seem to fall within one of three groups: one group which cannot produce an appropriate plural on either real or nonsense words, a second group which can produce an appropriate plural for each real word but cannot produce one for all or most of the nonsense words, and a third group which can produce appropriate plural forms for both all real words and all or most nonsense words. When the children were uncertain about an appropriate plural form, they frequently used a learned form, even if it required them to significantly alter the form of the singular word.

The children in both Berko's study and that of Graves and Koziol were monolingual. Diane and Luiz Natalicio studied native and nonnative speakers in grades one, two, three, and ten. Each of 24 final-consonant phonemes was paired with one of three initial consonant-vowel (CV) combinations (*pa-*, *su-*, *ni-*), resulting in a 24-trigram test instrument. In the 24 consonant phonemes there were three plural allomorphs: *-s* (as in bets), *-z* (as in beds), and *-ez* (as in matches). The Natalicio study found that for the male pupils studied, "native English speakers appear to continue to progress in the formation of English plurals through the third grade (where near-perfect performance occurs), and show no apparent change when tested in the tenth grade." The nonnative English speakers made comparable progress in the first two grades, but the level of their performance was inferior in the third grade. The authors felt that the unusually poor control over the plural inflection in English demonstrated by tenth-grade nonnative English speakers may indicate undue attention to assumed problems in the first two years of education, coupled with decreasing emphasis on oral language after the second grade. The result is the stifling of normal development of linguistic behavior.[7]

Moshe Anisfeld and G. Richard Tucker asked six-year-old children to give the plural for the singular form and to give the singular for the plural form of nonsense names of cartoon animals. Children made more errors with syllables requiring the addition or deletion of the *-ez* allomorph than with syllables requiring either *-s* or *-z*.[8]

How does the child acquire such rules? Presumably, he discerns patterns of regularity in the adult speech to which he is exposed and induces rules to account for these regularities. From the words, phrases, and sentences that he hears, he abstracts certain rules he uses until additional information causes him to revise them. This additional information may take the form of exposure to new vocabulary, experience with irregular sequences, or corrections by parents or teachers. He will modify his rules repeatedly to incorporate these new data, although a lag may exist between exposures to revelant data and active use of new rules based on those data.[9]

Because the child may not yet have been exposed to all pertinent linguistic information, his rules may be different from those of the adult community. Noam Chomsky has noted: "It is by no means obvious that a child of six has mastered this phonological system in full—he may not yet have been presented with all of the evidence that determines the general structure of the English sound pattern."[10] With regard to plurality, some investigators, for example, Susan Ervin and W. R. Miller, have suggested that a numeral preceding a noun may be construed by the young child as a sufficient marker of plurality, resulting in such constructions as *two book* and *one-two shoe.*[11]

Such observations suggest that any attempt to study the nature of the child's pluralization rules must focus on his knowledge not only of "adult" rules but also of any other rules he may adopt temporarily. There is some indication that the child at about the six-year level abstracts the general rule that pluralization involves lengthening the singular form.

LANGUAGE DEVELOPMENT
AND THE DISADVANTAGED CHILD

A major concern of modern American education is the coexistence within the schools of several different child populations. Probably nowhere is the crisis so acute as in the area of communication skills, of which grammar is the basic element. With the rapid theoretical advancements in linguistic science since the late 1950s, many materials have become obsolescent.

It has long been accepted that there are differences between standard and nonstandard varieties of speech. While there is general agreement that the disadvantaged child has a smaller vocabulary than his middle-class peers, it is debatable whether vocabulary size or syntax per se affects school learning. Not knowing five synonyms for beautiful or saying "he don't" is unlikely to impede school learning. What is more likely to interfere is the disadvantaged child's inability to use language to meet the demands of the school. When he is asked to follow directions, participate in discussion, compare two objects or events and make discriminations between them, classify, or draw inferences, he is often at a loss to do so. In a word, his inability to use school language is traceable to differences between the middle-class child and the disadvantaged child in terms of social and cultural experiences.

For the teacher of communication arts, dialect differences, whether regional or social, might well become a source of enrichment of the curriculum. A person's language is one of his most intimate possessions, something he associates with his family and friends and neighborhood. As such, it is to be respected by all who encounter it— especially in those situations in which a pupil may be called on to supplement his native variety of the language with another form of discourse for public occasions. As long as the situation is handled with respect for every person's speech-ways, there is no reason why the varieties of grammar, pronunciation, and vocabulary found in the classroom population should not be used to show that language, the most characteristic feature of human behavior, can come in a wide range of patterns.

Research on socially and emotionally disadvantaged children has consistently highlighted their retarded language development. Disadvantaged children are more likely to obtain lower vocabulary definition scores,[12] to speak in shorter sentences,[13] and to exhibit poorer pronunciation, articulation, and use of grammar.[14]

Several studies, for example the widely quoted work by Carl Bereiter and Siegfried Engelmann, have stated that the disadvantaged child does not use words in the same way as other children. A child from such a background does not construct sentences from words at all but rather from differently structured units, perhaps larger conceptual groupings.[15] It is also often noted that such children tend to omit certain words in their speech, for instance articles and prepositions.

But child language always differs qualitatively as well as quantitatively from adult language. The concept that disadvantaged children speak a primitive language is based on a false premise, because there is no evidence that primitive languages ever existed.[16] Few educators or linguists would want to suggest that disadvantaged American children speak something other than English or that their language differs enough from the standard to be considered a separate language.

One study which cited kindergarten and first-grade children re-telling a story just told to them used a task similar to "Show and Tell," which is commonly employed in the classroom situation. The impressive difference favoring the advantaged over the dis-advantaged children was in sheer verbal output rather than in retelling the essential features of the story. The telling of the story, "Curious George" (Hans A. Ray) by the adult and by each child was supported by the use of illustrations.[17] This, of course, was an aid in the sequential development of the story and in recalling details.

All forms of all languages are produced by regular rules, and this is true on all levels of language. Thus, disadvantaged children do not eliminate sounds at random but rather have a regular and fully describable set of rules by which they pronounce their language. The effect of some of these rules is to eliminate certain sounds, notably final consonants and consonant clusters, *r* and *l,* and some inter-vocalic nasals. Other rules function in determining the shape of vowels in these children's language. They may produce vowels that do not occur in the same context in standard English, for instance, *flow* for standard English *floor* (flɔr). But as noted in Chapter 5, young children in different dialect communities have identical grammars up to a point—they make the same kinds of errors with many of the identical words. In fact, they have learned the *structure* of their language so well that the school does not easily change it if it is "sub-standard," that is, if it deviates seriously from the prestige language of that society. Although the young child's vocabulary is meager, it is easy to add to it once he has internalized the underlying patterns that compose his language.

When the Indian child's lack of educational achievement is examined, a simple reason is found: Indians do not do well in school because of bilingualism and biculturalism. The Mexican-American's poor educational showing is also attributed to bilingualism. With the black child, the diagnosis is different. While the other two groups have too many languages, the black child does not have enough of one—that is, he does not have adequate language.

The black child's language appears to be his biggest handicap. He has been unable to express himself clearly and at length. When the typical black child was asked in one study if he knew how to play basketball, he responded, "Uh, uh," whereas the white middle-class child embellished and expanded his answer.[18] The black child's environment does not give him the perceptual and intellectual experiences essential for success in school and certainly not the language that accompanies and binds these experiences. As Martin Deutsch observes, "for these children language becomes an effective tool only when it has adequate feedback properties in communicating with peers or others who share the particular subculture."[19]

Susan Houston's studies support this theory in her identification of school and nonschool language style among 11-year-old blacks. In out-of-school activities the group of children engaged in language games, verbal contests, and narrative improvisations far removed from linguistic disability. Throughout the study the children showed expected syntactic patterns characteristic of children about 11 years of age. A far different style, the school language, was used with all persons perceived by the children as in authority over them and in formal and constrained situations.[20]

Language acquisition is not a skill, as participation in games may be considered a learned skill, except that children must hear a language in order to learn it. The language of the disadvantaged child is useful to him, systematic and regular in its rules of construction, and as good a base for thinking and conceptualization as any other form of language. He may lack some of the lexicon he needs in order to succeed in school, to read newspapers, and so forth. But all children must be taught items of syntax and semantics in which they are deficient.

THE CHILD AND HIS GRAMMAR

Normal fluent speech adheres to about five or six grammar rules per second. A teacher or other adult can seldom detect in a child's speech more than one conflict with standard grammar per ten seconds, on the average. And the one time he was "incorrect" feels no different to the child speaker than the 50 times he was "correct." Thus the child must feel every critical intervention or correction to be an unjustified interruption of his fluent speech.

To most children, school requires a whole new way of thinking, and it is unrelated to any real situation encountered elsewhere. Thus a child will accept the necessity of stacking blocks and following other commands which seem silly to him because school activities are designed for this purpose.

Teachers of the "new grammar" are encouraging experimentation with grammatical and derivational transformations. Through experimenting with the use of words, through generating sentences, the child is able to invent his own devices. Thus the teacher encourages and demonstrates sentence patterns, but the child selects those that his maturity level and his needs require.

SUGGESTIONS AND ACTIVITIES FOR THE COLLEGE STUDENT AND THE CLASSROOM TEACHER

1. Linguists and educators generally agree that the six-year-old child has knowledge of the structure of his language. If you accept this premise, how do you explain such slips as *breaked* for *broke* and *tooken* for *taken*?

2. The six-year-old child is able to use every part of speech and every form of sentence. Why is much of the child's time in the elementary school spent in selecting the correct verb or noun forms in a workbook? If you do not approve of workbooks, what methods and material would you use to help the child to improve his written sentence structure?

3. Set up a series of about 20 real and nonsense words which form plurals with an -s, or -z, or -ez allomorph. Secure the cooperation of two or more pupils in grades one, two, or three. Test one child at a time, giving him the singular form and asking him to give you the plural form. Tape-record the responses, and as a check ask another student to record them on paper. Discover for yourself the extent of mastery of pluralization rules.

4. Using some of your prepared material on singular and plural forms, select several pupils on one grade level. Give one child the singular forms of all the words in your series and ask him for the plurals. Give another child all the plural forms and ask him for the singular forms. Tape-record each word you give and the child's response. Also record each child's response on paper (if an unfamiliar form is given, write the response phonetically). The tape and the written record will be a check on the accuracy of your research.

5. Michael Graves and Stephen Koziol state that some pupils at the third-grade level show mastery of the appropriate plural form of real words and nonsense words and others show mastery of few,

if any, plurals for nonsense words.[21] What factors might contribute to this deficiency? Ideas for discussion might include limited language in the home, inability to transfer from "known to unknown" (real to nonsense words), lack of meaning in nonsense words.

6. At what age can the child gain greater amounts of information from simply listening to a story? Make up a story or find a story unfamiliar to a group of children. Adapt the procedures of Marion Blank and Sheldon Frank[22] to a group of children. Record your story and children's responses on tape for class analysis.

7. Nancy Suzuki and William Rohwer found that fifth-grade children learn the nouns in noun-verb-noun sequences faster than in noun-conjunction-noun sequences. Thus the pair *mop-saddle* was learned much faster in the context "the *mop* smashed the *saddle*" than in the context "the *mop* and the *saddle*."[23] Is this related to the meaning-making process? Can you set up some noun pairs with deep meaning and others with little emotional content to try out on children or college students?

8. Can you find support for either of the two following statements: *a.* Disadvantaged children speak a primitive language. *b.* Disadvantaged children have a regular set of rules for pronouncing their language.

9. Which point of view is more related to the study of language structure? What is your position on "nonstandard" English?

10. At the beginning of the school year, dialect differences are evident in any classroom. How can you use your knowledge of regional and social differences to enrich the curriculum and also instill a respect for each child's speech-ways?

11. How can you accept the many varieties of grammar and differences in pronunciation in your classroom without making a child feel self-conscious about his speech?

NOTES

1. R. W. Langacker, *Language and Its Structure* (New York: Harcourt, Brace and World, Inc., 1968, pp. 13–16.

2. Roger W. Brown and Colin Fraser, "The Acquisition of Syntax," *Child Development Monographs,* 39 (1964): 43–79. By permission of the Society for Research in Child Development.

3. Ragnar Rommetveit, *Words, Meanings, and Messages* (New York: Academic Press, 1968), pp. 254–55.

4. Martin Joos, "Language and the School Child," in *Language and Learning,* ed. Janet A. Emig (New York: Harcourt, Brace & World, Inc., 1966), p. 105.

5. J. Berko, "The Child's Learning of English Morphology," *Word,* 14 (1968): 150–77.

6. Michael F. Graves and Stephen Koziol, "Noun Plural Development in Primary Grade Children," *Child Development,* 42 (1971): 1165–73. By permission of the Society for Research in Child Development.

7. Diana S. and Luiz F. S. Natalicio, "A Comparative Study of English Pluralization by Native and Non-Native English Speakers," *Child Development,* 42 (1971): 1302–06. By permission of the Society for Research in Child Development.

8. Moshe Anisfeld and G. Richard Tucker, "English Pluralization Rules of Six-Year-Old Children," *Child Development,* 38 (1967): 1201–17. By permission of the Society for Research in Child Development.

9. Paula Menyuk, "Syntactic Rules Used by Children from Preschool through First Grade," *Child Development,* 35 (1964); 533–46. By permission of the Society for Research in Child Development.

10. Noam Chomsky, "Comments for Project Literacy Meeting," *Project Literacy Reports,* September 1964, pp. 1–8.

11. Susan M. Ervin and W. R. Miller, "Language Development," in *Child Psychology,* 62nd Yearbook of the National Society for the Study of Education, Part I, ed. Harold W. Stevenson (Chicago, University of Chicago Press, 1963), pp. 123–24.

12. V. P. John, "The Intellectual Development of Slum Children: Some Preliminary Findings," *American Journal of Orthopsychiatry,* 33 (1963): 813–22; Mildred C. Templin, *Certain Language Skills in Children* (Minneapolis: University of Minnesota Press, 1957).

13. John, "Intellectual Development of Slum Children."

14. D. H. Encroyd, "Negro Children and Language Arts," *Reading Teacher,* 21 (1968): 624–29.

15. Carl Bereiter and Siegfried Engelmann, *Teaching Disadvantaged Children in the Preschool* (Englewood Cliffs, N.J.: Prentice-Hall, Inc., 1966), p. 34.

16. E. H. Lenneberg, "The Capacity for Language Acquisition," in *The Structure of Language,* ed. J. A. Fodor and J. J. Katz (Englewood Cliffs, N.J.: Prentics-Hall, Inc., 1964), pp. 579–603.

17. Norman A. Milgram, Milton F. Shore, and Charlotte Malasky, "Linguistic and Thematic Variables in Recall of a Story by Disadvantaged Children," *Child Development,* 42 (1971): 637–40. By permission of the Society for Research in Child Development.

18. Bereiter and Engelmann, *Teaching Disadvantaged Children.*

19. Martin Deutsch, "The Role of Social Class in Language Development and Cognition," *American Journal of Orthopsychiatry,* 25 (1965): 78. Copyright 1965, The American Orthopsychiatric Association, Inc. Reproduced by permission.

20. Susan H. Houston, "A Sociolinguistic Consideration of the Black English of Children in Northern Florida," *Language,* 45 (1969): 599–607, and "A Reexamination of Some of the Assumptions about the Language of the Disadvantaged Child," *Child Development,* 41 (1970): 947-63. By permission of the Society for Research in Child Development.

21. Graves and Koziol, "Noun Plural Development."

22. Marion Blank and Sheldon M. Frank, "Story Recall in Kindergarten Children," *Child Development,* 42 (1971): 299–312.

23. Nancy Suzuki and William D. Rohwer, "Deep Structure in the Noun-Pair Learning of Children and Adults," *Child Development,* 40 (1969): 911–19.

PART THREE

Emphases in the New Grammar

Chapter 7

Words, Words, Words

WORDS ARE obviously essential, yet they are insufficient as ingredients of verbal messages. If words are spoken, they are temporal strings of phonemes, if they are written in English, they are spatial strings of graphemes.

Words have been examined under many conditions. They may be divided into such classes as abstract and concrete, but evidence shows that all words are abstract on one level. Moreover, the difference in levels is not a permanent characteristic of the words but varies with the way they are used. Thus *wealth* is likely to represent a higher level of abstraction than *dollar*. But if a few coins is your entire wealth at the moment, you probably consider *wealth* on the lowest verbal level. On the other hand, if you say, "He is always anxious to pick up an honest *dollar*," you are using *dollar* on a fairly high level. Nevertheless, since *dollar* is usually a low-level word, it will probably make a more direct and forceful impression on a hearer in most circumstances than *wealth* would.

From earliest times the symbols men have used to aid the process of thinking and to record their achievements have been a source of both wonder and illusion. The properties of words as instruments for the control of objects are impressive. All of the elaborate forms of social and intellectual life are affected by changes in our attitudes toward and our use of words.

The power of words can be a great force in one's life. Even words for which one has no real meaning can be used to illustrate an analogy, as the following example shows:

> *The gostak distims the doshes.* You do not know what this means; nor do I. But if we assume that it is English, we know that *the doshes are distimmed by the gostak.* We know too that *one distimmer of doshes is a gostak.* If, moreover, *the doshes are galloons,* we know that *some galloons are distimmed by the gostak.* And so we go on and so we often do go on.[1]

Words are the natural units of language. What is considered to be a word depends upon how the users of language feel about where the divisions between words should come. In English full-time employment is written as three words; in German it is written as one word. In thought this may be considered as one idea, but in the alphabetic writing of a language the habits of word separation persist.

ORIGINS OF WORDS

According to most linguists, it is impossible to trace a word to an absolute origin. Linguists seem to feel there is no solution to the problem of the precise nature of primitive speech.

If you look up the derivation of a word in the dictionary, you will usually find it traced back to some particular time in English (such as Old English or Middle English) and then listed as derived from Latin, Greek, French, German, Hebrew, or some other of the thousands of languages spoken on earth. Especially if it is a common word, it may be listed as of Old English origin, with nothing (or perhaps Gothic) before that. For most purposes there is little value in or need for tracing a word back more than one or two thousand years.

You may not care whether a word came from Gk. (Greek) or OHG (Old High German). However, a glance at the information given about the etymology often makes the word seem considerably more interesting and therefore easier to remember. Moreover, if you form the habit of examining the etymology of every word that interests you, you will soon begin to recognize parts of words and will thus be able to analyze many of them without using the dictionary at all.

Try analyzing words that interest you into their component parts. The examples *geometry* (a branch of mathematics), *biology* (the science of plants and animals), and *autograph* (signature) can be analyzed as follows:

geo=earth	metry=measurement
bio=life,	logy=science
auto=self	graph=write

Geometry began as a method of surveying or "earth measurement." Knowing that *bio* originally meant life will help you to find its significance in other connections, as in *biometry* (life measurement). After this introduction to word analysis you should be able to make a good guess about what *graphology* (writing science) and *autobiography* (self-life writing) mean.

OLD ENGLISH WORD USE

Old English poetry attains a remarkable flexibility through the wealth of synonyms for words like *war, warrior, shield, sword, battle, sea, ship*—sometimes as many as 30 for one of these ideas—and through the bold use of metaphor. The king is the leader of hosts, the giver of rings, the protector of evils, the victory-lord, the heroes' treasure-keeper. A sword is the product of files; the play of swords, a battle; the battle-seat, a saddle; the shield-bearer, a warrior. Warriors in their woven war-shirts, carrying battle-brand or war-shaft, form the iron-clad throng. A boat is the sea-wood, the wave-courser, the broad bosomed, the curved-stem, or the foamy-necked ship, and it travels over the whale-road, the sea-surge, the falling of waves, or simply the water's back. Synonyms never fail the author of Beowulf: Grendel is the grim spirit, the prowler on the wasteland, the lonely wanderer, the loathed one, the creature of evil, the fiend of Hell, the grim monster, the dark death-shadow, the worker of hate, the mad ravisher, the fell spoiler, the incarnation of a dozen other attributes characteristic of his enmity toward mankind. One cannot long remain in doubt about the rich and colorful character of the Old English vocabulary.[2]

The richness of English in synonyms is largely due to the happy mingling of Latin, French, and native elements. It has been said that there is a synonym at every level—popular, literary, and learned. Albert Baugh points out that a difference is often apparent, as in *rise-mount-ascend, ask-question-interrogate, goodness-virtue-probity, fast-firm-secure, fire-flame-conflagration, fear-terror-trepidation, holy-sacred-consecrated, time-age-epoch.* In each of these sets of three words the first is English, the second is from French, and the third from Latin. The difference in tone between the English and the French words is often slight; the Latin word is generally more bookish. However, it is more important to recognize the distinctive uses of each than to form prejudices in favor of one group above another.[3]

Resourcefulness of Old English Vocabulary

Before the borrowing of words from Latin and French, Old English of necessity developed unusual resourcefulness to convey meaning by bending old words to new uses. By means of prefixes and suffixes, a single root was made to yield a variety of derivatives. These were extended when compounds were formed.

The word *mōd,* which is our word *mood* (a mental state), meant in Old English 'heart', 'mind', 'spirit', and hence 'boldness' or 'courage', sometimes 'pride' or 'hautiness'. From it, by the addition of a common adjective ending, the adjective *mōdig* was formed with a similar range of meanings (spirited, bold, high-minded, arrogant, stiff-necked), and by means of further endings the adjective *mōdiglic* magnanimous, the adverb *mōdiglice* boldly, proudly, and the noun *mōdignes* magnanimity, pride. Another ending converted *mōdig* into a verb *mōdigian,* meaning to bear oneself proudly or exultantly, or sometimes, to be indignant, to rage. Other forms conveyed meanings whose relation to the root is easily perceived, *gemōdod* disposed, minded, *mōdfull* haughty, *mōdlĕas* spiritless.[4]

The root *mōd* lent itself to combining with other words meaning *mind* or *thought,* those that meant various mental states, such as *kindness, sorrow, proud.* From the same root more than 100 words were formed. Old English was resourceful in utilizing its native material, while Modern English relies more on its facility in borrowing and assimilating elements from other languages.

ATTEMPTS TO CHANGE VOCABULARY

Before the turn of the century every writer felt competent to "purify" the language by proscribing words and expressions because they were too old or too new, or were slang or cant or harsh sounding, or for no other reason than that he disliked them. One author objected to such expressions as *handling a subject, driving a bargain,* and *bolstering up an argument.* Another attacked *encroach, inculcate, purport, betwixt, methinks,* and *subject matter.* Questions were raised regarding the last term as to whether it was one or two words and what subject matter was meant. Most of the words criticized are still in use. It is futile to try to interfere with the natural course of linguistic history.

There were objections to foreign borrowings, especially French. At the time the French language was at the height of its prestige it was considered a necessary part of one's education. The concern was with turning English into French, rather than a refining of English by French. A number of words did not win permanent acceptance, but among those that have been retained are such useful words as *ballet, boulevard, chenille, coiffure, connoisseur, coquette, dentist, negligee, patrol, pique, routine, soubrette, syndicate.*

Borrowings from Other Languages

Studies have been made to determine what proportion of modern English is still composed of its basic Anglo-Saxon vocabulary and what proportion is borrowed words. In terms of dictionary entries, a count has indicated that only about one-fifth of the words in a dictionary are of Anglo-Saxon origin and three-fifths are either Greek or Latin in origin. According to Marshall Brown, this statistic would seem to indicate that English has ceased to be basically a Germanic language. But a more significant statistic is one which is based on the *commonly used* words. In this case, analysis of the 500 most commonly used words reveals that 72 percent are of Anglo-Saxon origin, whereas only 28 percent are of other origin. Of the 1,000 most frequently used words, according to Brown, the following percentages of words have come from various sources:[5]

Old English	61.7%	Mixed	1.3%
French	30.9	Uncertain	1.3

| Latin . . . . 2.9 | Low German |
| Scandinavian . . . . 1.7 | and Dutch . . . . 0.3 |

Paul Roberts agrees that some 62 percent of the thousand most common words in English are native English, but he points out that these high-frequency words are *the, of, I, and, because, mother, man, road,* and so on. Of the words in the *American College Dictionary,* only about 14 percent are native. But the modern vocabulary is very much Latinized and Frenchified.[6] Loanwords, once assimilated into the body of a language, serve as bases for further formations just as all other words do; for instance, the noun *chauffeur,* borrowed from French, is the basis for the verb *to chauffe* (as in *I had to chauffe my mother around all day*). A suffix like *-able,* originally used only in Latin or French loanwords like *inevitable, amiable,* has now become so general that it can be added to any English verb, as in such forms as *eatable, seeable, lovable.* The suffix *-able* has become one of the most widespread and productive English formative elements.

Sometimes borrowings took place so long ago or have become so familiar that the speakers of the language no longer recognize them as borrowings, as in the case of *chair* and *table* from the Latin. There is not and has not been for thousands of years any "pure" language, in the sense of one having no borrowings from a foreign language. You are all familiar with such foreign words in English as *sputnik, spaghetti, smorgasbord, chile con carne, fortissimo, au revoir.* You are perhaps less aware of the fact that many other words which seem completely familiar and form part of everyday usage also are of foreign origin.

When a standard language has been established, it often borrows forms from other dialects (regional, social, or occupational), for various reasons: distinctive meanings, humorous connotations, or to establish or avoid pleasant or unpleasant connotations of one sort or another. In America contact with the Indians, for example, resulted in a number of characteristic words such as *caribou, hickory, hominy, moccasin, moose, opossum, papoose, raccoon, squaw, tomahawk, totem, wampum, wigwam.*

Many more words have been derived from other parts of North and South America, especially where the Spanish and the Portuguese settled. Thus in English we have Mexican words such as *chili, chocolate, coyote, tomato.* From Cuba and the West Indies came *barbecue, cannibal, canoe, hammock, hurricane, maize, potato, tobacco,* and from Peru, *alpaca, condor, jerky, llama, pampas, puma, quinine.* Brazil and other South American regions were the source of such words as *buccaneer, cayenne, jaguar, petunia, poncho, tapioca.*

English contact with the East has been equally productive of new words. Words from India include *bandana, bangle, bengel, Brahman, bungalow, calico, cashmere, china, curry, juggernaut, jungle, jute, mandarin, pariah, polo, rajah, rupee, thug, toddy, tom-tom, verandah.* From a little farther east came *gingham, indigo, mango, seersucker,* the last an East Indian corruption of a Persian expression meaning "milk and sugar" applied to a striped linen material.

From Africa, either directly from the natives or from Dutch and Portuguese traders, such words as *banana, boorish, chimpanzee, gorilla, gumbo, palaver, coodoo, zebra* were obtained. Australia is the source of *boomerang* and *kangaroo,* words which have passed into native use. One of the reasons for the cosmopolitan character of the English vocabulary today is the multitude of contacts the English language has had with other tongues in widely scattered parts of the world.

WORD CREATION

At all periods in the history of a language a new word may suddenly appear as if from nowhere, or a word may be deliberately created by one man to tell the world exactly what he is doing or to advertise his product, as George Eastman's *Kodak* or Bernard Shaw's *Superman.* In 1833 the astronomer Sir John Herschel coined *periodicity* on a French model, and H. Piddington introduced *cyclone* in 1848 from a Greek word meaning "to go around." One of our most common words, *sandwich,* was named for John Montagu, the fourth Earl of Sandwich, who enjoyed this type of snack in the eighteenth century. The names of scientists are used as common nouns of measuring units in electricity: *ampere* from the French scientist A. M. Ampere; *watt* from James Watt, the English scientist. To have even one entry in the dictionary to their credit is an honor few men have achieved, although without doubt such creations have been made by numberless individuals whose contributions were never recorded.

Words from Initials

In the more than 600,000 entries in a modern unabridged dictionary, there are practically no words without some sort of source. A source of new words of growing importance consists of the initials or initial syllables of words. The stock example of such an "original" word is *Kodak,* which is said to have been manufactured by putting together a series of previously unrelated letters. Many commercial trade names are formed on this plan, as *Sacony* for Standard Oil Company of New York and *Ascap* to designate the American Society of Composers, Authors, and Publishers.

Women in the armed forces are designated by abbreviations that are used as words: *Wac, Wave, Spar. Radar* was coined from *radio direction and ranging,* and *loran* was made from *long-range navigation.* The "alphabet agencies" were a feature of the New Deal. In some instances one set of initials stood for two or more things: CCC meant Civilian Conservation Corps and also Commodity Credit Corporation, another governmental bureau; AAA could refer to either the Agricultural Adjustment Act or to the American Automobile Association. And millions of Americans never did learn the distinction between PWA (Public Works Administration) and WPA (Works Projects Administration).

These combinations of initials do not, of course, make words, but CAB (Civil Aeronautics Board) does. More recently the term CODAC appeared in the news media; this was coined from Community Organization for Drug Abuse Control. Every child is probably familiar with US (United States and UN (United Nations). The frequency with which some terms are noted in newspapers depends on their current activity, as noted in BIA (Bureau of Indian Affairs), HEW (Health, Education and Welfare), AA (Alcoholics Anonymous), or GM (General Motors).

Word Formation by Affixes

Affixing is the most frequently used of the grammatical processes. Among the three types of affixing—prefixes, suffixes, and infixes— suffixing is common. Suffixes probably do more of the formative work of language than all other methods combined.

Both prefixes and suffixes are bound forms. Any linguistic element that cannot be used as a word by itself is a bound form, as the *re-* and *-ed* in *re-entered* and the *un-* and *-ing* in *unhitching.* Affixes can alter in various ways the meanings of words to which they are attached. They may shift a word from one part of speech to another. Thus the adjectives *true* and *green* can be turned into nouns by adding the suffixes -*th* and -*ness*, to make *truth* and *greenness*. Thomas Hardy subdues language to his purposes when he writes verbs like "to unbe," "unillude," or "unbloom," and nouns like "unease" and "lippings" (meaning *talk*).

Suffixes are sometimes used to give words different meanings without changing their functional classification; for example, *gray* and *grayish*, both normally adjectives, and *man* and *manhood*, both normally nouns. More often suffixes convert words from one classification to another, as in the following examples:[7]

Verbs to nouns: appease-appeasement, serve-service
Adjectives to nouns: free-freedom, happy-happiness
Nouns to verbs: atom-atomize, gas-gasify
Adjectives to verbs: dark-darken, tranquil-tranquilize
Nouns to adjectives: child-childish, man-manly
Adjectives to adverbs: glad-gladly, frantic-frantically

This kind of conversion is common in many languages including Greek, Latin, and French, from which a great many English words come. It explains many of the related words in the language.

Word Formation by Compounding

Aside from borrowing, probably the greatest source of new words is the compounding or joining together of old ones. *Buttercup* is a different word from both *butter* and *cup; stepchild* is not the simple joining together that it seems to be, for the first syllable is the Old English *steop* (Modern English steep), which meant high, projecting, and hence unprotected. Compounds which are self-explanatory were prevalent in Old English, as they are in Modern German. In Modern English there is the borrowed word or a word made up of elements derived from Latin and Greek; examples are lamp (light + vessel), earring (ear + ring), and many more.

Compound words are composed of two or more free forms. Examples of single free forms are: *man, house, dog*. Compound words like *sailboat, sunrise, fallout* are composed of two free forms. Complex words are formed by combining free forms, sometimes slightly altered, with bound forms, as in *tru*th, *basket*ry, *happi*ness, *runn*ing, *manage*ment, *author*ity. Complex words can also be formed by combining bound forms with other bound forms, such as *in-trans-*

igen-cy, sup-ple-ment, and by combining bound forms with free forms, as in *thinker, thinking.*

Such English forms as *killjoy* and *marplot* illustrate the compounding of a verb and a noun, but the resulting word has a strictly nominal, not a verbal, function. It cannot be said that *he marplots.* Some languages allow the composition of all or nearly all types of elements. Edward Sapir states that the Indian language of the Paiutes, for instance, may compound noun with noun, adjective with noun, verb with noun to make a noun, noun with verb to make a verb, adverb with verb, or verb with verb.[8]

Verb Formation

According to Lincoln Barnett, Charles Ogden and Ivor Richards, while collaborating on *The Meaning of Meaning* (1936; 10th ed., 1952), found that a few hundred key words could do all the real work in their analyses of other words and idioms. They compiled what is known as Basic English—850 volatile, versatile words that can say anything about anything that needs to be said in ordinary talk. Their stripped-down lexicon requires only 18 verbs—as against the 4,000 to 10,000 that may be available in the vocabulary of a college-educated man. The 18 vital verbs are: *be, come, do, get, give, go, have, keep, let, make, may, put, say, see, seem, send, take,* and *will.* The ability of these verbs to do the work of all the others stems from their gift of entering into an astonishing number of mergers with prepositions. Thus a combination like *give up* can cover the pivotal meanings of *abandon, abdicate, adjure, cease, cede, desert, desist, discontinue, forego, foresake, relinquish, renounce, resign, sacrifice, stop, succumb, surrender, vacate, withdraw,* and *yield.*[9]

Baugh claims that 20 of the simplest verbs enter into 155 combinations leading to over 600 distinct meanings or uses. The verb-adverb combination which gives English a distinctive flavor results in *set out, bring about, catch on, give out, put up with, lay off, hold over.* Many of these groups are of colloquial or even slang origin—*dish out, crack down on.*[10]

Verbs often meet the hostility with which new words may be received, particularly by those who look into the history of language. Samuel Johnson, in his dictionary of 1855, described *to bamboozle* as "low" and *to wabble* as "low and barbarous." He also sought to put down *to coax, to budge, to fib, to swap,* and *to derange.* Most of these have been used in English for some time, but when writers dislike a word they give no heed to its history or its linguistic value. *To contact* flowed quite naturally out of the noun *contact.* It was first noted in a pamphlet concerning the duties of workers in the post office about 1924. There was much objection to its use in speech and writing, but *to contact* appeared in Webster's New International in 1934. By 1941 it was in wide use in the Army and Navy.

For centuries *to process* had existed in English as a law term. By the early 1920s it was applied to the canning of fruits and vegetables. But it was not until the 1940s that human beings were *processed,* and soon *to process* signified almost anything involving change. According to H. L. Mencken, the word has taken on all the shades of meaning of *examined, inspected, instructed, investigated, organized, registered, manipulated, studied, sorted, tested, screened, judged,* and *edited.*[11]

The embryologist of speech discerns several processes in the making of such novelties as *to rubberneck.* As H. L. Mencken notes:

Some are simply nouns unchanged, e.g., *to contact, to author, to style, to decision, to taxi, to pressure* and *to signature;* others are back-formations from nouns, e.g., *to locate, to enthuse, to reune, to resurrect, to intermiss, to aggravate, to liase, to vamp, to commute, to reminisce, to typewrite* and *to jell;* yet others are made by adding ancient suffixes to nouns common or proper, e.g., *to glamorize, to slenderize, to hospitalize, to simonize, to hooverize, to publicize, to finalize,* and *to funeralize. . .* ; or by prefixing a particle, e.g., *to entruck.* Again, there are new verbs made of old verbs, mainly with negative prefixes, e.g., *to debamboozle, to dewater* and *to disadmire.* Sometimes, yet again, the original word is neither a noun or a verb, but an adjective, as in *to thin, to peeve, to slim,* and *to safen,* or a preposition, as in *to up, to plus, to over,* or even a conjunction, as in *to if.*[12]

After nearly a quarter of a century of use, students may be interested in discovering which of the verbs Mencken cites are still in common use, which are no longer heard in conversation or found in print, and which forms, if any, are no longer listed in the dictionary.

Portmanteau Words

A telescoped word arbitrarily formed from two distinct words to make a humorous term is called a portmanteau word. An example is *cyclotron,* from *cycle* and *electron.* The term "portmanteau" originally was a description of a group of facetious words. It originated not with a linguist but with the mathematician-poet Lewis Carroll, who explained in *Through the Looking-Glass* that he had created words such as *chortle* and *galumph* by fitting two words into one, as clothes are fitted into a portmanteau or traveling bag. *Chortle,* from *chuckle* and *snort,* has become a permanent part of humorous English. But *slanguage (slang + language), insinuendo (insinuate + innuendo),* and numerous others which were originally for comic effect are limited in their general usefulness.

Gossip columnists are often particularly fertile in this sort of word coining. Some years ago Walter Winchell used *infanticipate* for *expect a baby* and *Renovate* for *obtain a divorce in Reno.* Earl Wilson suggested that useless talk be called *Congressation (Congress + conversation).*

Portmanteau words or blends have become a vital part of our vocabulary. Children enjoy discovering how some words are made: *smog* consists of *smoke* plus *fog, slithy* of *slimy* plus *lithe,* and *brunch* of *breakfast* plus *lunch.* Margaret Bryant lists such blends as *twirl, slide, flurry, flush, electrocute, dumbfound, scurry, splatter, flounder* (verb), *boost, flaunt, foist, grumble, squash.*[13] Mencken cites several other blends, including *Hobohemia (hobo-Bohemia), Hoovercrat* (a Democrat who voted for Hoover), *refugew (refugee-Jew), sneet (snow-sleet), sportcast (sport-broadcast),* and *radiotrician (radio-electrician).*[14] Developments in advanced electricity are referred to as *electronics* and those in the field of nuclear science as *nucleonics.*

Onomatopoeia

Words formed by onomatopoeia are old and extensive, yet such words still are being augmented by new creations. These are, as the Greek term says, onomatopoetic or "name-making," that is, "self-made" words. An alternative name is "echoic," because they echo the sound they name.

Gertrude Boyd has noted that onomatopoeia can also be the formation of a word, as *cuckoo* or *boom,* by imitation of a sound made by or associated with its referent. In representing a thing by a

word that sounds like it or the imitation of natural sounds, onomatopoeia relates sound to meaning. The child learns to appreciate such
words through the creation of effective sounds such as *hum, whiz,
zoom, crack, twitter, crackle, swish, jangle,* and *crunch.* Sleigh bells
usually *jingle* and *tinkle;* they do not *clatter* or *clang.*

Children like to listen to imaginary language and create their own
words in the manner of Laura E. Richards, who created "Rummy-
jums," "bogothy bogs," "loppoping Lizard," "a Glimmering Gog,"
and "Wiggledy wasticums," Mary O'Neill writes of fire as *hiss,
crackle, pop, whoosh, snap* and the sound of water as *slap, gurgle,
splash,* and Mary Austin gives her trains a chuck-a-luck, chuck-a-luck
movement.[15]

The word "pom-pom," dating from the Boer War, took a new lease
on life when naval vessels installed *pom-pom* guns to stave off attacks
by aircraft. In World War I, *whizz-bang* was supposed to "echo" the
sound made by a particular type of shell, and World War II produced
ack-ack, presumably portraying the sounds of antiaircraft guns,
which became known as *ack-ack* guns. There is an enormous number
of such words, many of them sound-imitative, which consist of
duplications with either change of vowel or change of the initial
consonant, as *sing-song, riff-raff, wishy-washy, harum-skarum, roly-
poly.*

For the young child the sound words Laura E. Richards uses in
"The Baby Goes to Boston" are appealing, such as the repetition of
jiggle joggle and the refrain of *Loky moky poky stoky/Smoky choky
chee,* a series of nonsensical words that is pleasing to the ear. Edward
Lear produces similar sound effects with *Pidy, Widy, Tidy, Nice-
insidy.*

The prevalence of reduplication or the repetition of all or part of
the radical element is natural. This process is used to indicate such
concepts as distribution, plurality, repetition, customary activity,
increase of size, added intensity, continuance. In English it is not
generally accounted one of the typical formative devices of the
language, however. Such words as *pooh-pooh* and *goody-goody* have
become accepted as part of the normal vocabulary, and the method of
duplication may on occasion be used more freely, as in *big, big man,*
or *Let it cool till it's thick thick.* Such usages are common, especially
in the speech of children. Sapir states that words of the onomatopoeic
type are all but universal. Examples are found in Russian, Tibetan,
Manchu, Hottentot, and Chinook.[16]

James Joyce experimented in the creation of new word forms to meet special needs. Onomatopoeia shaped some of the new formation of words. A long-held note of a song, a "longindying call," is said to dissolve in "endlessnessnessness"; a woman's hair is "wavy-avyeavyheavyeavyevyevy"; the sound of passing horses' hoofs becomes "steelhoofs ringhoof ring." Disjointed meditation is indicated by clipped forms: "He saved the situa. Tight trow. Brilliant ide," for "He saved the situation. Tight trousers. Brilliant idea." But it is noteworthy that the most audacious coiners of verbal currency are limited to units capable of conveying sense—and therefore meaningful because they are in some degree familiar.[17]

POPULAR AND LEARNED WORDS

Words may be classified in different ways. J. B. Greenough and George Kittredge classify them as popular and learned. They feel that in every cultivated language these classes comprise the whole vocabulary. Popular words are those one becomes acquainted with in ordinary conversation. Such words may be termed "popular," since they are the stock in trade of all who speak the language. The English language also includes a multitude of words which are comparatively seldom used in ordinary conversation. The first acquaintance with these is from such sources as books one reads and lectures one hears. Such words are called "learned." No two individuals have the same stock of words, and the same word may be popular in one man's vocabulary and learned in another's.[18]

Greenough and Kittredge say:

> When we call a word "popular," we do not mean that it is a favorite word, but simply that it belongs to the people as a whole—that is, it is everybody's word, not the possession of a limited number. When we call a word "learned," we do not mean that it is used by scholars alone, but simply that its presence in the English vocabulary is due to books and the cultivation of literature rather than to the actual needs of ordinary conversation.[19]

Note the contrast, in the "popular-learned" point of view, in the following pairs of synonyms: *same-identical, building-edifice, thin-emaciated, fat-corpulent, piece-fragment,* and *beggar-mendicant.*

Today's English

Several years ago *Newsweek* magazine featured a series of articles that discussed the problems caused by pollution of the environment.[20] As the following examples show, these articles placed great demands on the reader. In the course of several pages of text, these words occurred: *noxious, volatility, monolithic, quasi-governmental, herbivores, megalopolises, hydrologists, despoliation, apocalyptic.* In addition the articles contained phrases like these: *nuclear holocaust, photochemical oxidants, esthetic privation.* Many of these words and phrases—which are largely derived from the Latin and Greek—are new to our language because the concepts they express relate to new discoveries in science. But every literate person in our society is expected to understand them and the concepts that attend them.

Marshall Brown points out that mixed in with the difficult words in this series were phrases made up from a simpler vocabulary: *jet port, recycling system, heat pollution, petroleum cracking towers, frontier ethic, tank farms, catch basins.* The concepts in these phrases are not necessarily any easier to understand than those in the phrases listed above, but in most cases the vocabulary is within the grasp of the reader. To understand the phrases, one must know what a "jet" is, how "port" is used in this phrase today, what "cracking" is in the petroleum industry, what kinds of "tanks" make up "farms," and so on.[21]

It is the little words, however, that constitute a language within a language. Each one pinch-hits for hundreds of more complex if subtler words. But their simplicity is deceptive, and their very versatility can create confusion. The little word *up* can be used in so many ways. According to Lincoln Barnett, most of the time *up* behaves like a preposition, indicating direction (*He lives up the street*). But it can serve as an adverb (*It's time to get up*), a noun (*Every life has its ups and downs*), a verb (*I'll up you five dollars*), or an adjective (*The sun is up*). In addition to its multiple function in the combination *give up,* it plays a ubiquitous and sometimes superfluous role in a variety of other expressions, such as *add up, clean up, do up, drink up, hurry up, join up, line up, lock up, mop up, offer up, pay up, play up, ring up, set up, stop up, tie up, tidy up, wake up, wash up, work up, wrap up, up to now* and *up to you.* Then there are those situations where utterly unrelated concepts are evoked by one and the same phrase, for example, *make up,* whose transient meaning depends on whether the context is cosmetics (*She takes an hour to make up her face*), indecision (*I just can't make up my mind*), domesticity (*Let's make up the bed*), forgiveness (*Kiss and make up*), fiction (*I'll make up some kind of a story*) or atonement (*Some day I'll make up for this mistake*).[22]

Little words such as *up* are elusive words even for those who have lived and worked with them all their lives. In fact, the puzzles presented by prepositions confuse not only the foreign student but also those born to the English tongue, and most particularly those teachers and writers whose obligation it is to use them correctly.

English, for all its flaws and the difficulties encountered in it by foreign students, is being adopted everywhere by speakers of other languages. (see Margaret Bryant, *Modern English and Its Heritage,* or Mario Pei, *The Story of English.*) English has infiltrated other languages, and many English and American words are now completely international—not merely understood, but spoken and published around the world.

SUGGESTIONS AND ACTIVITIES FOR THE COLLEGE STUDENT AND THE CLASSROOM TEACHER

1. Select a few words commonly used in the elementary schools—in mathematics, music, science, spelling. Try to analyze them into their component parts. Then look up their etymology. What related words can you find and use?

2. Consult a history of the English language. Look for one-word synonyms (*beautiful - pretty*) and phrase synonyms (*a creature of evil—a worker of hate*). Which groups of synonyms do you feel would make your language more colorful? Do you prefer one word or a group of words? Try to add at least one synonym or one new word to your language each day.

3. Chapter 7 stated that the root *mōd* was the base for more than 100 words. Can you find other roots from which some or many words were formed?

4. List 100 common words you use daily, or find such a list.[23] Try to identify those words that are English and those that came from French, Latin, or Greek. In what category do the greatest number of words fall?

5. At various periods of the history of languages there have been

objections to foreign borrowings. At one time English speakers were concerned by the number of French words in their vocabulary. Have the French people or speakers of other languages added many English words to their languages? Examine newspapers and magazines written in other languages to locate printed English words. Listen to radio and television programs in other languages. Can you identify English words among those of another language?

6. If you are in or near a community in which another language such as Spanish, Indian, French, or German is spoken, try to discover what words have been added to the local speech from these languages. Tape record the spontaneous conversations of several age groups. Listen to local radio programs and check through local newspapers.

7. Form small groups of three to five of your classmates. Group 1 may try to create one or more new words or identify words recently noted in news media. Group 2 may list new words from initials. Group 3 may try making words by compounding.

8. Both Otto Jespersen and Anna Hatcher have been concerned with classifying noun compounds.[24] Both have found that there are many compounds which "do not fit anywhere." Minor problems within the classification might be writing the two words together, writing the two words with a hyphen, writing the compound as two words. How can you explain such differences to children? Do you agree on the compounding of broomstick, editor-writer, and morning mail? What changes might be made in writing these words?

9. Give each small group or committee in your class a word. Make up directions for using affixes to form new words. Groups may use all three types—prefixes, suffixes, and infixes—or only one type. Which type of affix can be used most frequently?

10. List words which show different forms of compounding. Are the numbers of compound words increasing? What unfamiliar compounds have you heard recently or seen in print?

11. Use common words such as *run, good, house* in phrases or sentences illustrating different meanings or parts of speech.

12. Make up or try to identify portmanteau words or blends which you can add to your vocabulary.

13. Search through poetry books or prose selections for

onomatopoetic words. Do you commonly use such words in your speech pattern?

14. Funk and Wagnall's *Standard College Dictionary* (1968) gives no less than 39 definitions of *run* as a verb, 18 as a noun, 4 as an adjective, and 8 idiomatic phrases in which the verb or noun *run* is used. This is a distressing situation in a language boasting of over a million words; it shows how overworked some of those words are, for lack of substitutes or perhaps of words as yet uncoined. How many synonyms and coined words and phrases can you list for *run*?

15. Practically speaking, English is the only language which has supported separate books of synonyms. Among those published in Roget's *Thesaurus* and books of synonyms and antonyms. Many words have dozens of meanings. In most languages there are few if any synonym books. How do you account for the need for substitutes or synonyms for many words in the English language?

NOTES

1. Adapted from Charles K. Ogden and Ivor A. Richards, *The Meaning of Meaning* (New York: Harcourt Brace Jovanovich, 1952), p. 46.

2. Albert C. Baugh, *A History of the English Language*, 2d ed. (New York: Appleton-Century-Crofts, 1957), p. 77. By permission of Prentice-Hall, Inc., Englewood Cliffs, New Jersey.

3. Ibid., pp. 225–26.

4. Ibid., p. 74.

5. Marshall L. Brown, *Language: The Origins of English* (Columbus, Ohio: Charles E. Merrill Publishing Co., 1971), p. 163. By permission of Charles E. Merrill Publishing Co.

6. Paul Roberts, *Understanding English* (New York: Harper & Bros., 1958), p. 39.

7. L. M. Myers and Gene Montague, *Guide to American English*, 5th ed. (Englewood Cliffs, N.J.: Prentice-Hall, Inc., 1972), p. 46.

8. Edward Sapir, *Language: An Introduction to the Study of Speech* (New York: Harcourt Brace Jovanovich, 1921), p. 67 as adapted.

9. Lincoln Barnett, *The Treasure of Our Tongue* (New York: Alfred A. Knopf, Inc., 1964), pp. 29-30.

10. Baugh, History of English Language, p. 402.

11. H. L. Mencken, "The Birth of New Verbs," in *Philologica: The Malone Anniversary Studies,* ed. Thomas A. Kirby and Henry Bosley Woolf (Baltimore: Johns Hopkins Press, 1949), p. 317.

12. Ibid., p. 317.

13. Margaret M. Bryant, *Modern English and Its Heritage,* 2d ed. (New York: The Macmillan Co., 1962), p. 316.

14. H. L. Mencken, *The American Language* (New York: Alfred A. Knopf, Inc., 1945), Supplement I, p. 326.

15. Gertrude A. Boyd, *Poetry in the Elementary School* (Columbus, Ohio: Charles E. Merrill Publishing Co., 1973), pp. 7–10.

16. Sapir, *Language,* p. 76.

17. Margaret Schlauch, *The Gift of Language* (New York: Dover Publications, Inc., 1.55), pp. 234–35.

18. J. B. Greenough and George Lyman Kittredge, *Words and Their Ways in English Speech* (New York: The Macmillan Co., 1961), pp. 19–28.

19. Ibid.

20. *Newsweek,* January 26, 1970, pp. 31–47.

21. Brown, *Language,* pp. 163–64.

22. Barnett, *Treasure of Our Tongue,* p. 31.

23. See Edward L. Thorndike and Irving Lorge, *Teacher's Word Book of 30,000 Words* (New York: Teacher's College, Bureau of Publications, 1944).

24. Otto Jespersen, *Essentials of English Grammar* (Tuscaloosa: University of Alabama Press, 1964); Anna G. Hatcher, "An Introduction to the Analysis of English Noun Compounds," *Word,* 12 (1960): 356–72.

Chapter 8

The Sentence

MORE THAN 200 different definitions of the sentence have been identified. The definitions of the English sentence usually found in the traditional grammars are based on meaning or upon meaning plus grammatical form. The familiar definition "A sentence is a group of words expressing a complete thought" does not furnish a workable set of criteria by which to recognize sentences. Nor does the statement that a sentence is a meaningful group of words containing a subject and verb describe what takes place in practical conversation.

THE SENTENCE DEFINED

Through the years much of the consideration given to the sentence in schools has centered upon the punctuation of written material. One source has noted that our only difficulty with complete sentences comes when we write. We usually speak in complete sentence units without much difficulty, but when we write, we have so many other things to think about that we get lost."[1]

Many teachers would disagree with this statement. Some will insist not only that conversation consists of sentence "fragments" but that one of the most important objectives of school English is to develop in students "the ability to speak, in conversation, in complete sentences, not in broken phrasing."[2]

Language arts teachers have devoted much of their attention to the sentences marked off by punctuation in their pupils' writing. Classroom discussion of the sentence has usually dealt with the types of sentences that appear in good prose. If fragmentary sentences were mentioned, it was always the examples of fragmentary sentences that appear in writing. The preoccupation of teachers with the rhetorical sentences of written composition rather than the grammatical sentences of living speech has been evident for many years.

Writers with a knowledge of linguistics have tended to define a sentence in relation to the spoken rather than the written form. Among the relevant definitions of the early 1930s are the following:

> The completeness or incompleteness of a communication is wholly a matter of intent or idea in the mind of the speaker.[3]

> A sentence is an utterance which makes just as long a communication as the speaker has intended to make before giving himself a rest.[4]

In an analysis of recorded speech by Charles Fries, the units of communication used were found to consist of the following types:

1. A single minimum free utterance. (*Tom has gone.*)
2. A single free utterance, but expanded, not minimum. (*Tom has gone, but he may come back.*)
3. A sequence of two or more free utterances. (*Tom has gone. He was here at 2 o'clock. He may come back.*)

These observations led to Fries's definition: "We start then with the assumption that a sentence . . . is a single free utterance, minimum or expanded; i.e., that it is 'free' in the sense that it is not included in any larger structure by means of a grammatical device.[5]

The word "utterance" appears frequently in linguistic discussions. The definition "an act of speech is an utterance" gives little indication of how much talk an utterance includes. The unit in conversation which is easiest to mark with certainty is the talk of one person until he ceases and another begins. This unit may be termed utterance.

In any language there are utterances which stand alone, which are separate from other utterances, which occur with silence before and after them. Fries so defines the sentence: "Each sentence is an independent linguistic form, not included by virtue of any grammatical construction in any larger linguistic form."[6]

THE SENTENCE AS A UNIT OF SPEECH

The sentence is the most important unit of English speech, even more important than the word. Exercising his imitative faculty, a child will attempt to babble whole sentences, however imperfectly.

Sentences are repeated from memory and are varied by analogy. Imagine, if you can, that all the sentences you have uttered during the past several weeks were recorded so that you could review them at leisure. You would find them to be surprisingly varied: long and short; simple, double, multiple, and complex; statements, commands, wishes, questions, and exclamations; balanced, periodic, and loose. The words have been largely of your own choosing, but the sentences have seldom been of your own making.

Basically the English sentence is two in one, a binary unit. The subject is that to which the speaker or writer wishes to draw the hearer's or reader's attention and the predicate is that which the speaker or writer has to say about the subject. Like the best writers, the best speakers can shape their sentences by word order in such a way as to give just the right degree of emphasis. Word order is becoming more significant as its use is recognized in providing the elasticity that gives the skillful speaker and writer all the scope and power he needs.

English-speaking people have inherited certain sentence patterns, but within those patterns there is great freedom to vary words, phrases, and clauses to obtain a simple or complex style. It is also possible to vary the vocabulary and speech level to suit the occasion and the needs and capacities of the hearers or readers.

Normally sentences are those multiword units of a message that give the feeling of having said something complete. The decision as to what a sentence is hinges on a psychological factor more than on any strict grammatical pattern. Thus sentences may be very short or very long, depending on how the user of the language feels about the proper length. They may also be constructed in a simple or complex manner. A sentence may be considered as any word or sequence of words which follows a customary grammatical pattern of a language and is felt to be a complete utterance.

SENTENCE TYPES

Sentences are sometimes classified as exclamatory (*Here it is!*), imperative (*Come here!*), interrogative (*Where are you?*), and declarative (*I am here.*). The great majority of all sentences are declarative. In fact, the structures of the other sentence types may be analyzed as declarative sentences rearranged for the special purposes of exclaiming, commanding, or questioning. But very often exclamations, commands, and questions omit the predicating verb, and declarative sentences, unless they answer spoken or implied questions (like *Where are you? Here!*) require the predicating verb to give the feeling of a complete utterance.

For example, as a sentence *He working* seems incomplete, for it lacks the predicating form of the verb—*is working* or *works.* Exclamations and questions, however, can be uttered without the predicating element, for example, *Hey, you over there! Which way?* This utterance would not be considered incomplete. As Hubert Alexander says:

> The imperative sentence, too, is different from the declarative, for it is indicated by a special form of the verb which can stand alone without the subject or doer being mentioned, as in "Look!" We may imagine, if we like, that the subject is understood, "You look!" However, this misses the feeling of the imperative and looks very much like a subterfuge to bring the imperative in line with the declarative form. Moreover, this principle of considering certain portions of an utterance to be understood raises other difficulties; all utterances leave some unsaid things to be supplied by the understanding of the listener.[7]

Perhaps sentences other than declarative should be required to be sufficiently meaningful, within whatever setting they occur, to give a satisfying sense of completeness. Where communication is involved the setting will in large part determine the sense of completeness because it is something that is shared by speaker and listener.

The dominant role played by the typical English declarative sentence is that of asserting or denying something, as *Cows are animals, Bill does not cut weeds.* What is asserted may be an action, *Bill cuts,* or it may be an attributed quality or condition, *Bill is tall.* But in either case there must be a subject, that is, someone or something to act or to be qualified. Thus the view of things can be organized into a set of minute dramas in which doers are doing and things are characterized by specified conditions.

In stressing the events rather than the actors and agents and recipients of action, verbs can be converted into verbal nouns of the gerund type. For example, the idea *They* ran *better today* could be expressed, as *Their* running *was better today.* Shifting the verb to a noun function by using a verbal noun throws emphasis upon the concept of running.

Sentences need other sentences to supplement their various meanings. There is always as much left unsaid as there is said, and there may be even more. And so groups of sentences accumulate into paragraphs and paragraphs into discourses. Beyond the words themselves, there are the contextual and tonal factors which also help to build the total meaning in language. Nevertheless, the sentence remains the central unit.

English sentence patterns show infinite variety. The best writers shape their sentences in such a way as to give just the right degree of emphasis, and this they must achieve, in written language, by word order alone. In spoken language, stress, rhythm, intonation, and pause make the meaning clearer. Within the sentence patterns of the English language there is abundant freedom to vary words, phrases, and clauses.

SENTENCE TRANSFORMATIONS
AND COMPREHENSION

For children to comprehend what they read, they must be able to understand the written language structures by which ideas, information, and concepts are conveyed. Although children may be fluent in their use of oral language and may have acquired control over the basic sentence patterns of the English language by the time they enter school, it does not follow that this fluency will automatically be transferred to written language structures.

Noam Chomsky has formulated the theory of transformational-generative grammar, which holds that every sentence can be represented on two levels, a surface level and a deep structure level. The surface level is the form of the language to which the learner is exposed—its spoken or printed form. The deep structure level allows the learner to understand the meaning of the sentence.[8]

For example, the sentences *John broke the window* and *It was John who broke the window* may be said to convey the same information, that is, to have the same meaning. Thus they would be similarly represented at the deep structure level. Their surface structure form (whether spoken or printed) would obviously be different. In line with this theory William Fagan states that the means by which sentence structures become more complex is the application of transformational rules—that is, the embedding or conjoining of various clauses, phrases, or even words.

Fagan tested pupils in grades four, five, and six to determine if reading comprehension was affected by the number or types of transformations in the language of the passages they read. Five categories including 43 transformations were identified by Fagan, as follows:

1. Embedding—a sentence enclosed within an existing sentence. For example, the appositive in *Bob Jones, a sailor, is home on leave.* (Bob Jones is a sailor.)
2. Conjoining—the union of two sentences by a conjunction. For example, *The room seemed lonely and* the room seemed *damp.*
3. Deletion—the elimination of words that would ordinarily appear in the surface structure. For example, the common-elements deletion in *The room seemed lonely and damp.*
4. Simple—transformations which act on a single existing sentence. For example, the negative in *He did* not *see the mirage on the desert.*
5. Position shift—in which either the sequential pattern of subject-predicate is inverted or various grammatical units are placed before the subject. For example, the adverbial position shift in *After a crash they always make pilots fly again.*[9]

A reader who misses a negative or a descriptive word within a sentence in a passage (a paragraph or longer, if conversation) may temporarily derive incorrect information. But further on in the passage another statement may correct the information. Thus the rapid reader may look back to an earlier statement to verify the later one or just alter his first impression to coincide with later developments.

Pupils should find it easier to understand what they read if they can analyze the various structures and understand the relationships of the various lexical items in the structures in the content read. In order to help build up a pupil's facility with printed language structure, Fagan suggests such exercises as the following:

1. Well-constructed sentences may be taken from various writings and divided into kernel sentences. Pupils then are asked to combine the kernels to form a single sentence. The various sentences produced may be written on the chalkboard or overhead projector for viewing by the class and comparison with the original sentences.
2. Pupils can be given complex sentences to break down into their component parts, indicating how the various parts are related.
3. Sentences which contain a number of referents (for instance, relative pronouns in sentences such as *The man who called left his telephone number)* can be used to ask pupils to replace all referents by the words to which they refer.
4. Pupils may be asked to list all the clues concerning a particular linguistic element named by the teacher. For example, the teacher may ask for all clues to the plurality of *huskies* in the sentence *The two huskies were the best friends Old Ootlik ever had.*
5. Sentence structures from children's writings (without identifying individuals who wrote them) can be used to ask pupils to suggest ways of improving or restating the sentence structures.[10]

SENTENCE TACTICS

Although the groundwork is laid in early childhood for the full development of native language skills, achievement in this area takes place during the whole period of childhood and adolescence. Any user of English is limited in the range of possible utterances he can form, not only by the extent of his vocabulary—the words he knows—but also by the number of structural options he has mastered. Most of the structural options he can exercise have been acquired through experience—the experience of his own speech community.

William Miller states that English syntactic structures result from three choices: choice of word, choice of word order, and choice of word form. As labels of abstracted bits of experience, words are selected, linked, arranged to communicate perceived relationships. *Word selection* is limited only by the extent of the vocabulary of the user, governed by the semantic considerations of appropriateness. *Word order* is limited to those structures known to the individual speaker or writer through his experience with and knowledge of language. *Word form* is the choice most strongly affected by classroom experience.[11]

In ordinary speech one seldom makes careful distinctions corresponding to standard written English. Inflectional suffixes are often slurred over, if pronounced at all, and many are difficult to hear even when they are pronounced. But the word is the basic unit of labeling, and the sentence is a basic unit of purpose. Although words are most often combined with other words in syntactic structures, it is possible for words to stand alone as complete utterances. There is a distinction between single words used to represent a predication (*Right!* representing *You're right* or *I agree*) and those used as an immediate expression of emotion (*Wow! Gee!*).[12]

SENTENCE USAGE

The most important division in the English sentence is still that between subject and predicate. The chief nominal form in the usual sentence, together with all its associated words (modifiers), is regarded as the subject or the thing talked about. The verbal form associated with it, together with all modifiers and complements, is the predicate. Since English has so few inflectional forms to indicate by suffix what function a word performs in a sentence, word order shows relationships. There is great difference between *The man bites the dog* and *The dog bites the man.*

Although formal grammars assert that every sentence must have a subject and a predicate, in actual usage phrasal locutions are complete and self-contained statements. Such exclamations as *The old boy himself!* have no particular verb "understood," but they are called presentative sentences. In announcing that *The child has a toothache,* the action is not contained in the verb *has,* but in the noun.

In the sentence, *It's a beautiful day, isn't it?* Margaret Schlauch states one actually means affirmation instead of negation in the latter part of the sentence; something like *You agree, I hope?* Whatever the historical origin of the illogical *Isn't it?* or *Don't you?* the words are contradictory. Note also the inconsistencies in using the present participial verb forms. *A crying child* means one who cries, but an *eating* or *cooking apple* is not one that eats or cooks, nor is a *hunting rifle* one that hunts. In a statement like *The streets were running with water,* one is trying to say that the *water* was running. In employing words like *would, could, should, might,* where power and desire are involved, one becomes involved in all sorts of polite evasions that end by reversing the sense of them. *Would you be so kind as to open the door?* really means *I know you are kind; therefore I do ask you to open the door.*[13]

SYNTAX AND THE YOUNG CHILD

Current research considers child language to be unique. Much of the research on this topic has been concerned with syntax and sentence formation. It has shown that even the young child's earliest two-word utterances are patterned in a specific way. Furthermore, all the basic structures used by adults to generate sentences can be found in the speech of nursery school children.

In her study of syntactic rules used by preschool, kindergarten, and first-grade children in free speech situations, Paula Menyuk found that children in kindergarten used all structures in a grammatically acceptable form at the phrase structure level of grammar.[14] (Phrase structure grammar includes the simple, active, declarative sentences of the language, such as *He goes, He goes home.*)

Nursery school children tended to use restricted forms of this type of sentence, such as *Read book, See a big car.* It was found that from two years ten months to seven years one month there was an almost steady rise in the percentage of children who used transformations. A transformation is a grammatical operation which changes a simple, active sentence into a passive construction, a question, a negative construction, and so on. For example, *Daddy goes* becomes *Daddy does not go* or *Did Daddy go?* through the application of certain transformational rules.

The young child's sentences usually consist of some combination of a content word such as verb, noun, adjective and a group of "function" words including articles, possessive pronouns, cardinal numbers, demonstrative adjectives or pronouns, quantifiers, and descriptive adjectives. The child uses relatively few function words but adds a large variety of content words in connection with the function words he does use. Once he knows a few function words he uses them with many different content words—nouns, adjectives. Thus, word meaning and syntactic skill are combined. The utterance or words used become a sentence as they acquire the status of words with specific functions and meanings as sentence segments. The child, therefore, gradually approximates adult grammar by building upon his condensed sentences.

All children are able to understand and construct sentences which they have never heard but which are nevertheless well formed. That is, they are well formed in terms of the general rules that are implicit in the sentences the child has heard. Somehow, every child processes the speech to which he is exposed so as to induce from it a latent structure. This latent rule structure is so general that a child can spin out its implications all his life long. It is both semantic and syntactic.

TEACHING SYNTAX TO CHILDREN

The teacher should be aware that the majority of studies on syntactic development are somewhat atypical, due to the fact that the children studied were quite verbal and intelligent. How much of the research in sentence development can be applied to the "normal" six-year-old is as yet unknown.

However, the teacher can benefit from some insights into the grammatical development of the child. The six-year-old child has mastered the basic rules for sentence formation, but he is not in command of the complete syntactic system. Armed with this knowledge, the teacher can build on the basic structures already established and introduce the child to the beauty and richness of our language through a variety of oral and listening experiences. To enrich the child's earlier acquisition of syntactical structure, a combination of listening experiences to both live and recorded sequential verbal utterances and participation in many types of oral expressions (dramatic play, planning sessions, games, songs) will enable the child to expand the syntactical system established in the preschool years.

Patterned Drill

The preschool program for disadvantaged four-year-old children developed by Carl Bereiter and Siegfried Engelmann relies upon

patterned drill, a method of teaching which has children repeat statement patterns. This program has been widely publicized, and it
should be well known.[15]

Language instruction in this program begins by teaching children
basic identity patterns by verbatim repetition. Typical material used
might be as follows:

1. *Verbatim repetition:*
   Teacher: This block is red. Say it.
   Children: This block is red.
2. *Yes-no questions:*
   Teacher: Is this block red?
   Children: No, this block is not red.
3. *Location tasks:*
   Teacher: Show me a block that is red.
   Children: This block is red.
4. *Statement production:*
   Teacher: Tell me about this piece of chalk.
   Children: This piece of chalk is red.
   Teacher: Tell me about what this piece of chalk is not.
   Children (ad lib): This piece of chalk is not green, . . . not blue,
      and so on.
5. *Deduction problems:*
   Teacher (with piece of chalk hidden in hand): This piece of chalk is
      not red. Do you know what color it is?
   Children: No. Maybe it is blue . . . maybe it is yellow . . .

Bereiter and Engelmann report that it takes four-year-old children
considerable time to learn these statement patterns, with their plural
variations and subclass nouns (for example, *This animal is a tiger*).
The length of time required varies from six or seven months for those
who came in with practically no spoken language, to two or three
months for those of near normal language competence. At the end of
this time the children can recite such statements as *If it's a hammer,
then it's a tool,* which purportedly illustrate efficiency in class
inclusion (knowing that *hammer* is a subclass in the more general
class *tool*) and in inferencing (knowing that *if* something is true, *then*
we can infer that something else is true).

Critics of such an approach to language training argue that the grammatical sentences children give are evidence of response learning. They also contend that it is too limited a program—the children are exposed to a very limited variety of syntactical forms, including a limited number of verbs, mostly in the present tense. With exposure to a rich vocabulary and a complex syntax in interactions with adults, children can process data and put together utterances they have never heard themselves. Celia Lavatelli points out that if a mother says to her three-year-old, "Find Daddy and tell him supper is ready," the child does not find his father and say, "Find Daddy and tell him supper is ready," as a child might parrot in patterned drill. Instead he says to his father, "Daddy, Mommy says supper's ready." Young children acquire structure of the language by listening to what is said to them, processing the information, figuring out the rules, and *using what they have figured out in reply.*[16]

Modeling

Modeling is a form of tutorial program. Working with a small group of preschool children, a tutor would reply to a child's utterances in a conversational manner and in doing so would model a rich variety of syntactical forms. The natural method of acquiring language is only useful if the child has sufficient chance to interact with adults who use language effectively.

Such a tutorial program would be highly desirable with children of limited language, since the usual classroom situation does not require overt responses by the child. In much of the classroom activity the teacher gives directions to which the child does not have to perform verbally and which he can carry out by imitating other pupils. In a one-to-one tutorial session, the teacher or other adult not only ensures that the child uses language, he can also plan the tutorial sessions to meet the special needs of the child. High school and college students serving as teachers' aids could carry on an effective tutoring program, with some training and guidance. Such a program would provide real-life experience for students interested in working with young children and would allow the experienced teacher time to develop a plan for evaluating the progress of each child.

When a small number of children, (four to six) are grouped around a table using crayons, puzzles, books, and so on, the teacher can carry on a conversation with more than one at a time. The number in a group and the interactions would depend upon age and the need for any one session.

DEVELOPMENT OF SENTENCE FORMS

The simplest way to ask a question is by intonation alone. Children start out by asking questions using intonation for question form.

Paula Menyuk and Nancy Bernholtz recorded the speech of one child who was producing primarily one-word utterances during the period between 18 and 20 months of age. They wanted to find out if various utterances of the single word *door* were simple repetitions of a name or if they were one-word (holophrastic) sentences with differentiated meanings:

> **That's a door. (declarative)**
> **Is that a door? (question)**
> **Shut the door! (emphatic)**

What the recorders or listeners considered to be declarative utterances ended with a falling frequency contour, questions ended with a rising contour, and emphatics rose sharply and then fell. Menyuk and Bernholtz concluded

> that the child's single word utterances are not simply names of objects and events and that the child uses prosodic features generatively (productively, or creatively according to rules) to create sentence types rather than merely imitating prosodic features or including these features as part of the speech sound composition of a particular word.[17]

Once children begin to put two words together, charting the development of mature sentence forms can begin.

CHILDREN'S USE OF QUESTIONS

The two most common types of questions are the yes-no questions: *Can the boy drive the car?* and the *Wh-* questions: *Where will he go?* If the first question is made into a simple declarative sentence (*The boy can drive the car*), that sentence can be divided into progressively smaller constituent units. Most English speakers would probably agree with the following sequence of divisions for this statement:

Sentence (S)
Noun phrase (NP) + verb phrase (VP)
Article (ART) + Noun (N) + auxiliary (AUX) + verb (VB) + ART + (N)

To convert this sentence into a question, only one transformation is required: The auxiliary *can* must be exchanged with the subject noun phrase, *The boy:*

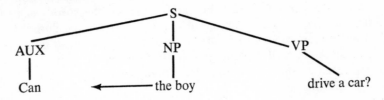

This process is called the interrogative transformation. Like all transformations, it can be applied to constituents of certain types here (NP + AUX), regardless of the particular words in that constituent in any particular sentence.

A *Wh-* question such as *Where is he going?* may be obtained from the declarative sentence *He is going somewhere.* To change the declarative to the interrogative, the appropriate question word (*where, when, what, who, which,* or *how*) has to be substituted for the indefinite pronoun *somewhere* and placed at the beginning of the sentence. Courtney Cazden states that this process is called the preposition transformation; in this example, it yields *Where is he going?* Applying the same transformation required for the yes-no question—transposing the auxiliary (here a form of *to be*) and the subject noun phrase—results in the final form *Where is he going?* Thus, whereas yes-no questions require only one transformation, *Wh-* questions require two.[18]

The Functions of Questions for Children

Children not only learn *how* to ask questions, they also learn *when* to do so. In fact, to look at when children ask questions means to look at the functions of language in human interaction. According to M. M. Lewis, questions serve the unique function of requesting a verbal response from another person. They invite participation in verbal exploration of the world. Sometimes the young child's questions seem a kind of verbal play; at other times, they are requests for confirmation of something already known or at least hypothesized, or requests for information that is entirely new. *Where* questions may be used instead of *when* in referring to temporal matters.

The chief result of obtaining replies to his *Where-* questions is this, that the child finds that through these questions he can take the initiative in causing another person to refer to something within their common environment and yet beyond the immediate situation. By securing social cooperation of this kind, he extends his area of reference, building up a structure of symbolization of what is absent.[19]

The Role of Questions in Education

When teachers listen to how children talk and what they say, they are better able to plan educational programs with child language in mind. With respect to questions, this has two quite different aspects: (1) attempts to teach children to ask more productive questions, and (2) attempts to change what happens in classrooms so that more of children's learning will be based on questions that they themselves ask rather than on questions asked by the teacher. A specific curriculum in inquiry training should be of greatest value in classrooms where children have plenty of opportunity to ask questions about topics of interest to them and to use these questions as the basis for their school work.

Recognizing the strong trend toward more student initiative and responsibility in directing their own learning, Dorothy Haupt examined the chain of teaching-learning episodes which start with a nursery school child's spontaneous questions. Haupt concludes:

The tendency of the nursery school teachers of the limited sample to reinforce their position as the prime verbal source of information and their limited use of reciprocal questions or leading open-ended responses suggests that frequently their acts of teaching are not consciously designed to provoke thinking on the part of the children. . . . The teacher's behavior does not encourage an orderly sequence of questioning utilizing either the child's past experiences or the abilities of other children to have followed the thread of a story, for example. . . . If children are to learn how to learn to pose relevant questions, and gain skill in handling increasingly complex thought processes, these require teachers who ask thoughtful questions and stimulate reflection and thinking. They need teachers who are able to pace their teaching acts from simple descriptive, factual responses to responses which guide the child's search for understanding of processes, progression, causality, classification and so forth.[20]

THE ACQUISITION OF SENTENCE VOICE

Children tend to develop the active-voice sentence earlier than the passive-voice sentence. Studies indicate that preschool children find it difficult to imitate passive sentences such as *His hair has been cut.* A form which was quite frequently substituted for this in the child's imitation was *Hair been cut.*

Active- and passive-voice forms are equivalent but alternate vehicles or means of expressing the same content. Differences between two sentences (for example, *The ball hit the boy* and *The boy was hit by the ball*) are: (1) total number of words in the sentence, (2) word order or the relationship between the semantic "actor" and "acted-upon" elements and the syntactic "subject" and "object" elements, (3) the form of the verb used, and (4) transformational complexity in terms of Noam Chomsky's grammar.[21]

Elizabeth Turner and Ragnar Rommetveit tested children four to nine years old on their ability to discriminate the sentence or name which went with a picture. The sentences were presented orally, and the children responded with "right name" or "name which goes with picture" rather than with "yes" or "no". Children were instructed that only one name went with each picture and were given such choices as *The fly catches the frog* and *The frog catches the fly.* They were able to respond correctly more frequently to active-voice sentences than to passive-voice sentences. Correct responses became more consistent with increasing age.[22]

Peter Herriot added several features to the experimental materials to test children five to nine years old. He used the simple perfect-tense affirmative active transitive sentence and its passive form: for example, *The boy has hit the girl* and *The girl has been hit by the boy.* Nonsense words were substituted in some of the sentence frames: *The boy has hit the girl* became *The boy has simed the girl, The kif has hit the jat, The guv has fuded the kif,* and their passive forms. Black ink pictures of boys and girls were shown for all statements. For sentences that substituted nonsense words children were told that the experimenter was going "to say a very strange thing," and they should listen carefully. At age three children could distinguish subject and object when given a semantically regular verb (*bumped*). For the nonsense sentences the difficulty was localized in the verb, that is, fitting the picture to the sentence containing a nonsense verb.[23]

Such studies have meaning for teachers and adults working with children from nursery school through the elementary grades. These adults must become more aware of the sentences they use to tell stories, give directions, explain terms. They also can note the sentences used by children—the simplicity or complexity for the age level. Fragments of free play, dramatization, or discussion can be taped for later analysis, in the early grades by adults and at higher levels by pupils and adults together. This can be carried further by examining sentences in books read *to* children as well as those read *by* children to ascertain the number of passive-voice sentences children fail to comprehend.

SUGGESTIONS AND ACTIVITIES FOR THE COLLEGE STUDENT AND THE CLASSROOM TEACHER

1. Word order is limited to those structures known to the individual speaker or writer through his experience with and knowledge of language. His main resource is his speech community (home, neighborhood). William Miller states that language resources acquired through this experience are regarded by the native speaker to be the norm; thus variations between the speaker's usage and standard English are considered to be the deviation of standard English from the norm.[24] Can you find support for this statement? Do you feel that deviation from standard English is "substandard"? What norm, if any, should be accepted?

2. Research has shown that exposure to adult models has a salutary effect on language development. If the language spoken in the home is nonstandard, or non-English, syntactic flexibility and control in English may well be impeded as a result. Recognizing that the quality and quantity of adult communication in English are crucial for the linguistic development of children, what can you do in your classroom and in the community to enable children to speak standard English when the occasion demands?

3. Bereiter and Engelmann use the methods of the patterned drills advocated by teachers of second languages.[25] In introducing statements involving polar concepts, they use the *not* statement; *This line is not long.* They then explain that there is another way of saying *not long:* "When a line is not long, we say that it is short. This line is short. Say it." Would you prefer to have children listen to recordings of standard English and literary selections, both

prose and poetry, rather than to use patterned drill?

4. As students begin writing paragraphs they must learn the relationships between sentences. A common use is that of a personal pronoun as a substitute word, as in the example: "Not long ago people thought of the *moon* as a thing. Now people think of *it* as a place." Do you feel that such links as articles, conjunctions, and prepositional phrases which show movement from sentence to sentence should be demonstrated as a point of clarification in writing? Do you feel that students need to learn about sentence connectives as soon as they begin to write more than one sentence?

5. The importance of groupings of words in speaking and in reading is known. List five common groupings heard in the speech of others and five from children's readers or communication arts textbooks. Make as many transformations as possible with these groupings, as in active to passive, assertion to negation, present to past or future.

6. Select some of the word groups in the preceding activity or make up other word groups. Use these as illustrations of sentence-modifier constructions, placing the modifying word groups in different parts of the sentence.

7. Secure or draw pictures of activities involving a boy and a girl, as a boy hitting a girl, a boy playing ball with a girl, and a boy running toward a girl. Be sure that there are clear indications as to which is the boy and which is the girl.

   Then make up several sentences as *The boy has hit the girl, The girl has been hit by the boy.* Make other sentences on the same patterns using nonsense words for *girl, boy,* and the verb, as *The boy has simed the girl, The guv has fuded the kif.* After you have made a dozen or more sentences try out your experiment on one or more children ages five to nine. Read each sentence twice and ask the child to indicate which of the pictures fits what you said.

8. Make up pairs of figures in black ink on white cards using squares, rectangles, or elliptical circles. Clearly indicate which is the boy (trousers) and which the girl (skirt). Use the same sentences made up for the experiment above with these figures and try your experiment on children and adults.[26]

9. Native speakers of English acquire their language resources in two categories: vocabulary and syntactic structures. Vocabulary acquisition comes first; words are learned—stored in the memory as

"labels" for recognizable bits of experience. The acquisition of syntactic structures occurs next, at the point where two words are put together as an utterance in such a way that one of the words is used to *say something* about the other. Are these two categories separate entities? Do they overlap? Are they mutually supportive? Give examples showing how they continue throughout life.

NOTES

1. F. G. Walcott, C. D. Thorpe, and S. P. Savage, *Growth in Thought and Expression* (Chicago: Benjamin H. Sanborn & Co., 19406, p. 34.

2. C. S. Pendleton, *The Social Objectives of School English* (Nashville, Tenn.: Tennessee Book Co., 1924), p. 36.

3. Janet Rankin Aiken, *A New Plan of English Grammar* (New York: Henry Holt & Co., 1933), p. 14.

4. Allan H. Gardiner, *Theory of Speech and Language,* 2d ed. (Oxford: Clarendon Press, 1951), p. 208.

5. Charles Carpenter Fries, *The Structure of English* (New York: Harcourt Brace Jovanovich, Inc., 1952), p. 25.

6. Ibid., p. 21.

7. Hubert G. Alexander, *Meaning in Language* (Glenview, Ill.: Scott, Foresman & Co., 1969), p. 79.

8. Noam Chomsky, *Aspects of the Theory of Syntax* (Cambridge, Mass.: The M.I.T. Press, 1965). Reprinted from *Aspects of the Theory of Syntax* by Noam Chomsky by permission of the MIT Press, Cambridge, Mass.

9. Adapted from William T. Fagan, "Transformation and Comprehension," *Reading Teacher,* 25 (1971): 169–72. Reprinted with permission of William T. Fagan and the International Reading Association.

10. Adapted from Ibid., p. 172.

11. William Miller, "New Sentencs Tactics through Predication," *College Composition and Communication,* 22 (December 1971): 365–76.

12. Ibid.

13. Margaret Schlauch, *The Gift of Language* (New York: Dover Publications, Inc., 1955), pp. 142–43.

14. Paula Menyuk, "Syntactic Rules Used by Children from Preschool through First Grade," *Child Development,* 35 (1964): 533–46. By permission of the Society for Research in Child Development.

15. Carl Bereiter and Siegfried Engelmann, *Teaching Disadvantaged Children in the Preschool* (Englewood Cliffs, N.J.: Prentice-Hall, Inc., 1966).

16. Celia Stendler Lavatelli, "An Approach to Language Learning," *Young Children,* 24 (1969); 373. Reprinted from *Young Children,* Vol. 24, No. 6, September 1969. Copyright © 1969, National Association for the Education of Young Children, 1834 Connecticut Ave., N.W., Washington, D.C. 20009.

17. Paula Menyuk and Nancy Bernholtz, *Prosodic Features and Children's Language Production,* Quarterly Progress Report No. 93, Research Laboratory of Electronics, Massachusetts Institute of Technology, Cambridge, Mass., April 15, 1969, p. 219.

18. Courtney B. Cazden, "Children's Questions: Their Forms, Functions, and Roles in Education," *Young Children,* 25 (1970): 204.

19. Morris M. Lewis, *Language, Thought and Personality* (New York: Harrap, 1964), p. 92.

20. Dorothy Haupt, "Teacher-Child Interaction: A Study of the Relationships between Child-Initiated Questions and Nursery School Teacher Behaviors," Ph.D. diss., Wayne State University, Detroit, 1966, pp. 288–89.

21. Elizabeth Ann Turner and Ragnar Rommetveit, "The Acquisition of Sentence Voice and Reversibility," *Child Development, 38 (1967): 650.* By permission of the Society for Research in Child Development.

22. Ibid., pp. 649-60.

23. Peter Herriot, "The Comprehension of Syntax," *Child Development,* 39 (1968): 277–78. By permission of the Society for Research in Child Development.

24. Miller, "New Sentence Tactics."

25. Bereiter and Engelmann, *Teaching Disadvantaged Children.*

26. See Herriot, "Comprehension of Syntax."

Chapter 9

The Role of Semantics

THE STUDY OF SEMANTICS can do more to help individuals become perceptive and sophisticated users of language than any other form of language study. Language is the medium through which all human sensory input is filtered and organized and in which most meanings are codified. It is language, because of its ability to represent ideas and to aid their development, that largely accounts for the intellectual superiority of men over animals.

LANGUAGE HAS MEANING

Language is used in human society for the purposes of communication. Hence, it has meaning, which is what gives it both its usefulness and its reason for existence. Because language comprises the basic vehicle for meaning-making and the communication of meaning among human beings, attention to the meaning-making processes in the teaching of communication arts is of great importance.

Meaning-making may also be referred to as "critical thinking," which has long been claimed to be one of the major objectives in the teaching of reading and communication arts. Research, however, does not verify the accomplishment of such skills in the elementary curriculum.

The meaning of any specific linguistic form is purely arbitrary. There is no underlying connection, no inherent or inescapable, relationship, between any linguistic form and what it signifies. Robert A. Hall, Jr., states that the same animal is referred to in English as *dog*, in French as *chien*, in German as *hund*, and so on. From the standpoint of logic there is no relationship between any of these combinations of sounds and the animal *canis familiaris* to which they all refer. The meaning of words is determined by the usage of the speakers of a language. It is wholly a matter of social convention. Different languages use the same combinations of sounds with entirely different meanings: the English word *do* means *perform, act* and is a verb, whereas the French *doux* (pronounced almost exactly like English *do*) is an adjective meaning *sweet,* and the German *du* is the second person singular pronoun meaning *thou, you.*[1]

Theory of Definition

Symbolization is the simplest, most fundamental way of defining. If one is asked what "orange" refers to, one may point to some object which is orange and say " 'Orange' is the symbol which stands for this." This merely says that "orange" is applicable in a single case, however. It is also necessary to know how it is applicable in general and to have the definition extended so it covers all the referents for which "orange" is a suitable symbol. Such generalizations can be extended to all types of definitions by the use of similarity relations. One may say "Orange applies to this and to all things similar to this as regards color." In practice the discrimination of one similarity relation from others generally requires the use of parallel instances, analogies in fact of the simplest order.

Thus similarity can be used as a defining relation. One can define the symbol "orange" by referring to something which is orange and saying "The symbol 'orange' is applicable to anything which is like this thing in respect to color."

SEMANTICS AND LINGUISTICS

Perhaps the most important branch of linguistics is semantics. In general, semantics is concerned with problems of meaning; the word is derived from "meaning" or "to signify." Semantics probably originated when man first became aware that he was using language as his primary mode of codifying and communicating meaning.

The most influential work on semantics has been *Language in Thought and Action*,[2] originally written by S. I. Hayakawa as his doctoral dissertation at the University of Wisconsin. It was used as a textbook in college freshman English courses and was subsequently selected by the Book-of-the Month Club, thus reaching a wide audience. Today it is probably the most frequently used book in both high school and college courses dealing with semantics.

From the beginning semantics was based on science. The kind of language characteristically used in science provided a useful model of how to keep verbal symbols in close correspondence with observable, verifiable events in reality. Apparently, what one can "see" is not only affected by the language one uses but is in fact determined by language, and scientists seem to be aware of the role that language plays in scientific enterprises. Scientists are concerned with language and the way in which it affects how one sees, thinks, and behaves.

Closer attention is being paid to the effects of language in different fields. Karl Menninger, in *The Vital Balance*, describes recent innovations in medicine as follows:

> Diagnosis is changing because we are changing our concepts of illness and disease. . . . We often speak in figurative terms of "fighting the disease," "facing it," of having a cancer, or suffering from arthritis, or of being afflicted with high blood pressure. . . . It is sometimes true that disease is an invasion; in other instances it is just as true that disease is not an invasion. . . . Illness is in part what the world has done to a victim, but in a larger part it is what the victim has done with his world, and with himself.[3]

There is accumulating evidence that medical diagnosis can cause a physiological condition. Human suggestibility expressed in physiological responses to verbal symbols has long been manifested in what is commonly called hypnosis.

THE MEANING OF MEANING

The function of language is to express and elicit meanings. Meaning is inherent in the very definition of language. In communicating with others, in teaching others about communication, meaning is the chief concern.

In trying to arrive at a meaning for meaning, David Berlo suggests the analysis of several English sentences to "see if we can abstract some commonality from them." The examples he suggests are as follows:

1. To use words properly, you must know what they mean.
2. The purpose of some writing is to communicate meanings.
3. I hear thunder. That means rain soon.
4. In English, the letter "s" at the end of the noun usually means "more than one" or "plural".
5. My family means much to me.
6. Words do not have meaning—only people do.

The first sentence implies that meanings are the properties of words, to be memorized when the word is learned. In the third sentence, the word "meaning" seems to indicate that one thing leads to another—in this case, thunder leads to rain. In sentence 5, the writer apparently is telling us the state of his feelings when he thinks of his family. Finally, sentence 6 says that meanings are not found in words at all; they are found only in people.[4] The uses of the word "meaning" in the sentences above, therefore, are not the same, and some of them seem inconsistent with the others.

Can a word have a meaning? Words are only scratches of ink on paper, speech is only a set of sounds that are transmitted through the air. Berlo's thesis is that meanings are not in messages, that meaning is not something which is discoverable, that words do not really mean anything at all, that dictionaries do not and cannot provide meanings. He states, rather, that *meanings are in people,* that meanings are covert responses, contained within the human organism. Meanings are learned, added to, distorted, forgotten, and changed. To the extent that two people have similar meanings, they can communicate. If they have no similarities in meaning between them, they cannot do so.[5]

There are several implications to the theory that meanings are in people: Meanings are the internal responses that people make to stimuli. Therefore, people can have similar meanings only to the extent that they have had similar experiences. Meanings are never fixed; as experience changes, meanings change. Because no two persons have ever learned the same word under exactly the same circumstances, each word has a special context for each individual. No two people have exactly the same meaning for anything. Sometimes people do not even have similar meanings. But whatever the situation, people will always respond to a stimulus in light of their own experiences. Communication at best is a compromise, for each person talks out of his own private world: his experiences, memories, impressions.

To understand the meaning of a word it is necessary to view the word from different aspects. One such method is by linguistic usage. Some individuals believe a knowledge of the usage of language alone is sufficient to know what a phrase means. But examine the following remarks:

1. They *meant* no harm.
2. He *means* well.
3. I *meant* to go.
4. What I *meant* was what I said.
5. A mechanistic universe is without *meaning*.

Note that in cases where the word "intend" can be substituted for "mean" (as is usually the case when these phrases are used), there is a quite different kind of "meaning" from any involved when "intention" cannot be so substituted.

And then there are those who confuse the sense of reference with the sense of intention in such phrases as *What I meant was, What I intended to refer to was,* or *What I intended you to refer to was.* In these cases there is still more confusion.

The verb *to mean* can usually be used as a synonym for the verb *to intend;* for example, *I didn't mean to do that, I didn't intend to do that.* The verb *to mean* dignifies "to have in mind," and an intention is in the nature of a proposed plan of action—something one has in mind to do.

The intention of the speaker can be used to illustrate the complex definitions of meaning for special purposes. To quote from an article in the early 1920s:

Is the meaning of a sentence that which is in the mind of the speaker at the moment of utterance or that which is in the mind of the listener at the moment of audition? Neither, I think.

Certainly not that which is in the mind of the listener, for he may utterly misconstrue the speaker's purpose. But also not that which is in the mind of the speaker, for he may intentionally veil in his utterance the thoughts which are in his brain, and this, of course, he could not do if the meaning of the utterance were precisely that which he held in his brain. I think the following formulation will meet the case: The meaning of any utterance is what the speaker intends to be understood from it by the listener.[6]

Kinds of Meaning

L. M. Myers identifies three kinds of meaning. When a man speaks, he uses words as symbols to indicate something that is going on *in his own mind.* His words are directly connected not with the processes in the outer world but with his own abstractions from those processes. It is this private mental activity that the words msan to *him,* and it can be called *meaning 1.* When another man listens, the words stimulate some activity in *his* mind. This activity can be called *meaning 2.* Meaning 1 and meaning 2 are so similar that there is little apparent difference, but the two meanings can never be absolutely identical. When there is an obvious difference between two meanings, it may be useful to consider which is closer to the *general habits of association;* this can be called *meaning 3.* The labels used for objects, as *paper, pencil,* are not "real" meanings, as *words in themselves have no meanings at all.* It takes a mind to develop a meaning by associating a symbol with something else, and no two minds work in quite the same way.[7]

If you find a puzzling word in a sentence and look it up, a dictionary can tell you something about how other people have used this word in the past. This information will give you a definite impression about what the writer means by the word in the sentence. Thus you learn something from the writer that you might otherwise have missed. But you cannot find the true and permanent meaning of the word, because there is no such thing.

Meaning-Making

James R. Squire found students were suffering from illiteracy in meaning-making. He summarized the results of his study as follows:

A study of the transcripts of student responses reveals six sources of difficulty to be particularly widespread among these 52 adolescent readers: the reader fails to grasp the most obvious meanings of the author; the reader relies on stock responses when faced with a seemingly familiar situation; the reader is "happiness bound"; the reader approaches literature with certain critical predispositions; the reader is sidetracked by irrelevant associations; and the reader is determined to achieve certainty in interpretation and is unwilling to hold judgment in abeyance. Other causes of difficulty occur, but these are the most common. Because the four stories were selected as representative of much fiction that is included in anthologies for ninth- and tenth-graders, the six sources of difficulty in interpretation may well represent fairly widespread reading problems of adolescents in this age group.[8]

A knowledge of semantics would improve the ability of students to "interpret" or make viable meanings of such stories because they would learn that one does not "get" or "grasp" meaning from words. One can only ascribe meanings.

MEANING IN THE COMMUNICATION PROCESS

Hubert Alexander identifies the phases of the communication process as four kinds of meaning: (1) the meaning as intended—*intentional meaning;* (2) meaning as the content of our message—*content meaning;* (3) the meaning of our signs and symbols, including language—*significative meaning;* and (4) meaning as interpreted by the receiver of a message—*interpreted meaning.*[9]

The content of most messages for most people will consist of the ideas they wish to convey. Ideas do not exist in a vacuum; they are closely involved with feeling qualities. An example is the use of the verb *to feel* rather than the verb *to think* in the expression *I feel this is a good plan.* Content meaning, therefore, is what one *intends* to convey, what one has in mind to express and communicate.

Significative meanings are always dependent upon the ways in which they are interpreted. Interpretations can vary from person to person and occasion to occasion. The particular context in which a word is used affects and modifies its verbal meaning. And over a period of time words tend to change their meanings—slang with short fads of meaning and well-established words over longer periods of time.

In receiving a message in the form of spoken words or written marks, one must first identify these sounds or marks as symbols that are supposed to have meaning. Then one must interpret the symbols to discover their meanings. If someone shouts an order such as *Forward, march!* the hearer cannot execute the command until he has first interpreted the words conceptually. The hearer must also first interpret an emotive expression like *My, what a beautiful rainbow!* in terms of the conceptual meaning of such words as *beautiful* and *rainbow.* Only then can he understand enough of the message to begin to sense the specific feeling that is expressed.

In interpreting spoken sounds or written marks, a degree of mis-interpretation is always possible. Intentional meanings are all too often changed or garbled when they are interpreted. One of the reasons for this is the different background experiences and cor-responding frames of reference held by the persons involved in a communicative process.

Major Words and Minor Words

The words that carry the key meaning of a sentence may be called major or content words, and others may be termed minor or structure words. Content words are those that carry most of the content of an utterance, whereas structure words are those (like prepositions, con-junctions, copulative verbs, adverbs, articles) that do most of the interconnecting and minor qualifying. Thus the major words provide the prominent characteristics of the situation which the sentence describes, and minor words fill in the background details.

As an illustration consider the following phrase composed only of minor words, *deliberately her into the.* Obviously something is lacking. The message is in the major words, *Mrs. Jones pushed cart mud.* To get the full import of the message one must put the major and minor words together: *Mrs. Jones deliberately pushed her cart into the mud.* Major words, usually the nouns and verbs, carry the burden of the lexical or independent word meaning. Minor or structure words are not only connectors, they contribute syntactical meanings and also lexical increments of their own. Thus in this example, the minor words tell you that the cart was pushed into the mud *deliberately,* not accidentally; that it was *her* cart, not someone else's; that it was *into* the mud, not out of it; and that it was *the* mud, one already mentioned.

DEVELOPMENT OF WORD MEANINGS IN THE CHILD

The preverbal infant perceives a verbal label as one of a multitude of attributes of an object (shape, weight, color, name). By the repeated association of seeing and touching the object and hearing the name of the object or person, the child acquires a bond between word and referent. The words thus learned are embedded in a sentence (the verbal context), and their referents (the objects to be paired with these words) are surrounded by a multitude of extraneous features in the environment. Learning words requires selective attention—the inhibition of irrelevant aspects of the learning environment.

Early experimental studies of semantic generalization show that adult speakers respond to linguistic stimuli as semantic entities rather than perceptual forms. As the child acquires language there appears to be a shift from the expression system level to the meaning system level in the processing of linguistic stimuli: Words emerge out of word forms as the child begins to attend to encoded messages rather than perceptual forms as such.

Heinz Werner and Bernard Kaplan maintain that such utterances as *Doll!* which dominate at an early stage of language acquisition are neither words nor sentences, but "monoremes" out of which both words and sentences emerge by means of a process of decontextualization. The characteristic feature of the early "monoremic" stage of the word form is thus a peculiar fusion of processes which later will branch off into referential, emotive, and associative part processes.[10]

A common noun such as *cup* may acquire many different references which emerge out of relationships between utterances including *cup* and a set of particular events. For one thing, other noncup objects like bowls, glasses, and cans are used in the same kind of activities; the noun *cup* thus becomes associated with the process of drinking. L. S. Vygotsky labels such associations "chain complexes." There may be many situations in which the two word forms *cup* and *drink* are uttered in the child's environment, so that overlap rather than separation seems to be the rule.[11]

A matrix of sentences in which two-word forms occur, however, provides the child with some basis for a distinction. Both *drink* and *cup* occur in slots like *I want a..........., The..........fell from the ledge.* Only *cup will appear in contexts like My..........broke, I shall wash your.......... .* And only *drink* will appear in contexts like *Father wants to..........his coffee.*[12]

Thus the reference of *cup* is intimately related to drinking behavior. But the word form *cup* is related to the object, and *drink* is related to the activity. A pattern of intricate mutual dependence within pairs of word forms is often reflected in dictionaries. A dictionary definition may define *cup* as "small, open container for beverages, usually bowl-shaped and with a handle." But *cup* in this sense does not include reference to *drink*. The separation of object from activity suggests other references such as *pour* and *wash* which can be associated with *cup*.

Word Meaning Patterns and Language Acquisition

S. M. Ervin and G. Foster examined the use of some adjectives among children in the first and sixth grades. The children were asked to use the adjectives *heavy, big,* and *strong* to describe a set of objects, and the words *happy, good,* and *pretty* were to be used to describe the drawings of a girl's face. The younger children used the adjectives in a less differentiated manner: *Heavy, big,* and *strong* were used more synonymously by first graders than by sixth graders. The age change was even more marked for *happy, good,* and *pretty*. The majority of the younger group used these three word forms synonymously in their descriptions. The authors suggested that "what remains as a connotative, metaphorical relationship in adults may in many cases start as a denotative nondifferentiation."[13]

The triad *happy, good,* and *pretty* is emotively nearly synonymous, whereas *happy* and *pretty* have distinct and different referential functions. The fact that they were used indiscriminately by most young children, however, indicates that such referential functions may not yet be firmly established at this stage. It also indicates that young children probably hear the indiscriminate use of descriptive words both at home and at school.

In another study of word meanings, Ragnar Rommetveit and V. K. Hundeide asked children at ages 9, 11, and 13 to sort sets of words, and they were also unexpectedly asked to reproduce some such sets of stimulus words from memory. One particular set contained the Norwegian words for *hospital, squirrel, cottage, wolf, crocodile, castle, rat, villa, hovel, butterfly, pussycat,* and *prison.* With the latter two words (*pussycat,* "a good animal," and *prison,* "a bad building") given as cue words, the list could be split into two halves in two different ways. The child could either sort out, as similar to *pussycat,* all *good* words, irrespective of reference (*squirrel, cottage, castle, villa, butterfly*), or he could pick all words for animals, irrespective of the emotive meaning or emotional quality (*squirrel, wolf, crocodile, rat, butterfly*). Younger children sorted words according to emotive meaning, while older children might readily switch strategies. Children who sorted the list into good versus bad words were able to reproduce fewer of the original stimulus words than those who sorted on the basis of reference. Sorting on the basis of reference facilitates recall by restricting active search in memory to a delimited subset of acquired vocabulary.[14]

SEMANTICS AND THE TEACHER

For the teacher of communication arts, semantics can be defined as the study of language operations in real human contexts, with emphasis on the human consequences of these "operations." According to Charles Weingartner this definition places *meaning* (or, more precisely, the processes of meaning-making) at the center of language study, with meaning being determined on the basis of the human behavior (and its consequences) that a specific language situation produces.[15]

In other words, meaning lies in the behavior of the language user. One begins speaking as one thinks and ends up thinking as one speaks. And, in turn, one behaves as one thinks. From the point of view defined here, any deliberate use of language that produces an intended response would be "correct." This definition distinguishes semantics from grammar by examining language as a process in actual human contacts rather than as signs and symbols, or as prescriptions and proscriptions intended to preserve some arbitrary notion of "correctness."

So semantics may be viewed as the study of the relations between language, thought, and behavior: how one talks, therefore how one thinks, and therefore how one acts. When the concern is how one talks, it is pointed toward one's own utterances. How one thinks and evaluates is inextricably bound up with how one talks. Most of thought is a matter of talking to oneself silently. If one's spoken words are hasty and ill-considered, it is likely that one's unspoken words are even more so. How one acts is determined by how one thinks. When one acts without thinking, the actions are likely to follow the lines laid down by the patterns of thought, which in turn are determined by the language one uses.

In teaching it is basic to discover whether you and your pupils are referring to the same things with the words you use. The first necessity in discovering whether pupils understand your language is to remember that the past histories of individuals differ. It is probable that their reactions to and use of any general word will vary. There will be some to whom a word is merely a stimulus to the utterance of other words, without the occurrence of any reference. These children respond to words much as they might respond to the first notes of a tune which they proceed to complete almost automatically. At the other extreme are those for whom every word used symbolizes a definite and completely articulated reference.

Normally whenever one hears anything said one springs spontaneously to the immediate conclusion that the speaker is referring to what one would be referring to were one speaking the words oneself. In some cases this interpretation may be correct. The support of gesture language can be helpful. Whenever words cannot be directly allied and supported with gestures, they are a very imperfect means of communication.

SUGGESTIONS AND ACTIVITIES FOR THE COLLEGE STUDENT AND THE CLASSROOM TEACHER

1. Consult several dictionaries and books on linguistics for definitions of semantics. Compare them with those given in this chapter. Make up your own definition. In pairs or small groups, defend your definition.
2. Discuss the difference between "getting" meaning from words and "ascribing" meaning to words. Do you feel that the "reading problems" of the typical adolescent are related to meaning-making problems? What other factors are involved?

3. Currently semantics is not a part of most curricula. To be included as a part of English, semantics will probably have to displace grammar. If you taught semantics in your elementary classroom, how would you develop interest in learning about word meaning to express ideas? Is this a different kind of "word meaning" than that referred to in developmental reading?

4. In a rapidly and constantly changing environment, data that demand that one make meaning of them can be almost literally endless. What criteria can you set up for selection of data or news media which will be of importance to you? Do your criteria tend to limit the kinds of information you would analyze?

5. Euphemisms and taboos in language provoke stimulating discussions as they relate not only to the English language but to other languages of the world. Gather examples in speech patterns and in literary sources. Note that one is no longer buried in "a graveyard" but in a "cemetery" or a "memorial park." The man who picks up the trash or garbage is no longer the "trashman" or "garbageman" but the "sanitary engineer," and one is no longer "poor" but "culturally deprived," "underprivileged," or "disadvantaged."

6. In the field of general semantics there is the incontrovertible fact that words *do not* have meaning, only people who use them do. That is, "I can only talk about what something is to me." Such statements question most traditionally accepted attitudes toward language and word meaning. (Read S. I. Hayakawa's Language in Thought and Action.) Hayakawa says we "react to words as if they *were the thing!*" In describing or defining a pencil, a pencil may be attached to a card with the word *pencil* lettered on it. But the *word* is not the thing, the letters p e n c i l are not the pencil. Select any common object and begin with the reasoning as with the pencil. What other lines of reasoning can you use? Can you explain your reasoning to others?

7. General semantics questions most traditionally accepted attitudes toward language, distorted advertising, media violence. Can you reconcile the meanings of the general semanticists and those of a dictionary or a glossary in a textbook?

8. The concept that "we must unlearn dead concepts" is itself new. No real future shock was experienced in the 1920s and 1930s with the changes made in methods and materials in the elementary

schools because new practices were rarely rapid and generally were extensions and refinements of familiar ideas, methods, or procedures. How does the scene of the 1970s differ, with its basic changes or innovations involving unfamiliar technologies or based on concepts with little or no precedent?

9. Can you accept the theory that meanings are in people? If you can, then perhaps you support the theory that no two persons have exactly the same meaning for anything. Thus our perceptions of things come from within us. They are the internal responses we make to stimuli. Can you explain your understanding of the idea that meanings are in people to a classmate? To a child?

10. A rain shower will cause some people to head for shelter, others to enjoy a brisk walk, and still others to express joy for an abundant harvest. How does our perception of an event affect our interpretation of that event, as the rain shower? How does meaning-making cause differences in the interpretation of directions, examination questions, legal documents? Are you willing to accept the concept of questioning in the meaning-making process called "learning how to learn"? Can you apply this concept to your own learning? to that of pupils in your classroom?

NOTES

1. Robert A. Hall, Jr., *Linguistics and Your Language,* rev. ed. (Garden City, N.Y.: Doubleday & Co., Inc., 1950), p. 124.

2. S. I. Hayakawa, *Language in Thought and Action,* 3rd ed. (New York: Harcourt Brace Jovanovich, Inc., 1972).

3. Karl Menninger et al., *The Vital Balance: The Life Process in Mental Health Illness* (New York: Viking Press, 1963), pp. 41–42.

4. David K. Berlo, *The Process of Communication: An Introduction to Theory and Practice* (New York: Holt, Rinehart & Winston, Inc., 1960), pp. 173–74.

5. Ibid., p. 176.

6. Alan H. Gardner, "The Definition of the Word and the Sentence," *British Journal of Psychology,* Cambridge University Press, 12 (1922): 361.

7. L. M. Myers, *Guide to American English,* 4th ed., © 1968 (Englewood Cliffs, N.J.: Prentice-Hall, Inc., 1968), pp. 146–47. By permission of Prentice-Hall, Inc., Englewood Cliffs, New Jersey.

8. James R. Squire, *The Responses of Adolescents While Reading Four Short Stories,* Research Report No. 2 (Champaign; Ill.: National Council of Teachers of English, 1964), p. 37.

9. Hubert G. Alexander, *Meaning in Language* (Glenview, Ill.: Scott, Foresman & Co., 1969), p. 6.

10. Heinz Werner and Bernard Kaplan, *Symbol Formation* (New York: John Wiley & Sons, Inc., 1963).

11. L. S. Vygotsky, *Thought and Language* (New York: John Wiley & Sons, Inc., 1962), p. 64.

12. Ragnar Rommetveit, *Words, Meanings, and Messages* (New York: Academic Press, 1968), p. 125.

13. S. M. Ervin and George Foster, "The Development of Meaning in Children's Descriptive Terms," *Journal of Abnormal and Social Psychology,* 61 (1960): 271–75.

14. Ragnar Rommetveit and V. K. Hundeide, "Emotive and Representational Components of Meaning in Word Sorting and Recall," *Pedagogisk Forskning,* 11 (1967): 47–59. Reported in Rommetveit, Words, Meanings and Messages, p. 128.

15. Charles Weingartner, "Semantics: What and Why," *English Journal,* 58 (November 1969): 1214.

Chapter 10

Grammar in a New Key

In the 1950s there was a turning point in American education. Among the new developments was the beginning of a movement for curriculum reform, in which the leadership largely has been directed to mathematics and the sciences. In all areas of the curriculum, however, the familiar organization of subject matter and methods has increasingly been questioned. Integrated curricula are continuing to be worked out for subjects that had long been kept separate. More attention is being given to the scientific method and the application of proven results in research and experimentation. Methods and materials are being based on current scientific information rather than that available a generation or more ago.

STRUCTURE AND SYSTEM IN LANGUAGE

Although the movement for curriculum reform in the communication arts is lagging far behind that in the sciences and mathematics, a revolution in grammar has been in the making for more than a decade. A fundamental of this new curriculum is that language has structure and system, and grammar is the study of structure and system in one of its most significant aspects.

The new grammar was developed in a series of steps. Surveys of errors led to observation and study of usage. This in turn raised the question of criteria for correctness, which led into a movement for a "new grammar." As more questions are raised the study of our language becomes broader and deeper.

Teaching by Example

In the kindergarten and early grades teachers write as children dictate. Composing and editing play a part in what the teacher actually records.

In the teaching of writing and any other language skill, one must write about something. One cannot write writing, any more than one can read reading. One can only write (just as one can only read) history, or geography, or science, or some other subject about which writing can be done.

Although it is recognized in the new curriculum that one should teach by example at all levels, teachers of communication arts do not appear to utilize the principle to any extent. They tell the pupil how to write, show him examples of what has been written, and after he has written something himself, they tell him how it should have been written. It is practically unknown in elementary or high school for the pupil to witness examples of anything *being* written.

There are few, if any, examples of the process of writing in language arts texts. There are only examples of something already written. Teachers themselves must provide the examples of how writing is done to demonstrate the process. To do this you could, the day before a writing assignment, write a story, a poem, or a report as you expect the pupils to write. Better still, find a quiet corner in the classroom and write your story as the children are writing theirs. After those pupils who wish to do so have shared their writing efforts, share yours with the class.

Grammar and Language

Because grammar is a system, it must deal with structure. That language has structure and system is fundamental to the study of grammar. Grammar as it has been known in American schools has been too narrow in scope, too shallow, too isolated from other disciplines to serve in a new curriculum.

A generation or two ago the place of grammar in the curriculum varied from school to school. It was practically eliminated from some elementary schools and remained strong in others. In some schools the teaching of grammar was begun in the early grades; in others it was reserved for the high school years.

The grammar test of yesteryear was a comfort to generations of American parents, pupils, and teachers. Such tests measured the pupil's mastery of a systematic description of English sentences. The basics included sentence types, parts of speech, and phrases and clauses. Pupils who went on to study French or Latin in high school found this grammar useful in identifying and classifying parts of an English sentence and in building sentences, especially in Latin.

CONSIDERATION OF DIALECTS

The term "dialect," as the linguist uses it, is neutral. It means any of the mutually comprehensible regional and social varieties of which a natural language consists. From the point of view of the dialectologist, everyone in a speech community speaks some dialect of his language.

A dialect is composed of a number of idiolects or subdialects. American English and British English are two large geographic dialects of present-day English, and each of these is made up of a number of more restricted regional dialects. Each regional dialect in turn consists of several more localized varieties or subdialects. Within a relatively large subdialect area like that of greater New York, which is part of the Eastern Seaboard dialect region, a number of localized varieties can be discerned; the speech of the Bronx is not precisely identical with that of Brooklyn, for example. And the same pattern of subdivisions within subdivisions holds true for the social dimension of dialects. Pushed far enough, dialectology encompasses many subtle distinctions.[1]

In the United States no single dialect has achieved the undisputed position of a *prestige dialect,* as was the case in England, where the upper-class speech of London and its vicinity came to be so regarded hundreds of years ago. Usually the prestige dialect is that of the social or cultural area of a region. In early colonial times the speech of Boston and vicinity was looked up to as a prestige dialect, at least by many New Englanders. But this claim was disputed by Virginians and other commercial and cultural centers such as New York and Philadelphia. Today there are a number of cultural centers which are spreading their influence.

Although speakers of English can understand one another, they do not all speak alike. Among the several hundred million native speakers of English there are many differences of pronunciation, grammar, and vocabulary. All speakers show their regional origin when they talk. It is not slovenly or substandard for a child from the near South to say "cain't" and "haow" and "tin cints." These are pronunciations used by millions of people, including educated people, in what the dialectologist calls the South Midland area and parts of the South.

An American who wants to get along professionally and socially among his educated fellow countrymen will do well to use the socially acceptable speech patterns that are standard for his area. All speakers of English reveal their social and educational position, often their occupation, in their vocabulary and pronunciation.

Some effort is being made (though greater emphasis is needed) to include consideration of dialect at all grade levels beyond the primary years. In addition there is need for study of the social implications of language, of linguistic history, and other related topics. The subject of grammar is being broadened to comprise a comprehensive and integrated treatment of language.

EMPHASIS ON ERRORS

For many years there was a belief that a standard of grammatical correctness existed. Some grammar textbooks set out to define what is "correct English" and what is "incorrect English." The public (and many teachers) wanted materials that would shoulder the responsibility of preserving a standard for speaking and writing.

Grammar was generally believed to be indispensable for "correct English," and every parent coveted correctness for his children. It was an accepted premise that language teaching should help eliminate errors in language use. Teaching was focused on those specific points of greatest value for this purpose, that is, on the rules that would be antidotes to the most common and serious errors. Mistakes in children's writing were collected, tabulated, and interpreted statistically in order to guide curriculum planners and classroom teachers in placing proper emphasis.

At no time in the history of English can any investigator find a time or a place where all the polite, educated elite employed exactly the same usages. On the contrary, volume after volume has criticized the grammatical "errors" of the great authors and men of distinction of the previous generation. Apparently the only ones who ever spoke correct English were the authors of the books condemning their predecessors and contemporaries for gross errors, and, of course, no two of them agreed with each other!

Language arts courses in schools and colleges can do more than give drill on questionable choices among common alternatives, demanding that one be taken as right and others as wrong. They can also provide practice in reading and writing, so children are taught to read and write for the ideas involved.

STANDARD AND NONSTANDARD ENGLISH

Written English is more standardized than speech, for it has long been subject to the emendations of editors, the restrictive injunctions of style manuals and handbooks, and the standards imposed by teachers and other authorities. Scholars sometimes refer the English that appears in reputable books and periodicals as edited English; it may be regarded as another dialect of the language, generally more conservative than spoken dialects.

There are, of course, varieties of written English; some writings are more literary than others, some are more scientific and technical, some are more scholarly and formal, and so on. These varieties may be classed as functional, for their characteristics are largely determined by the use to which the language is being put in them.

Present-day English, whether spoken or written, is divisible into standard and nonstandard levels, and within each of these levels there are, in both speech and writing, a number of functional varieties, ranging from very formal to highly informal. Standard English, written or spoken, is the version characteristically used by educated, cultured people, especially in the conduct of public affairs of various sorts; it generally avoids provincial, local, and eccentric expressions and constructions. But it may be very colloquial—that is, conversational and hence informal. The degree of formality it shows will be the degree that is appropriate to the use to which it is being put.[2] Nonstandard English, written or spoken, includes every other kind of English; it is generally characteristic of relatively uneducated people.

Within the standard and substandard levels there are words that have certain connotations or special meanings for one or more speakers. Each of us has some words which convey a special flavor for us alone. Analysts of meaning distinguish between *denotation,* or the meaning a form has for all those who use it, and *connotation,* or the special additional meaning the same form may have for some speakers.

Of the more widespread connotations, perhaps the most common are those that ascribe words to cultural (social) levels and to functional varieties. A form like *ain't* or *I seen* has the same denotation as *isn't* or *I saw,* but quite a different connotation: Many people think that the first pair connotes undesirable characteristics on the part of the speaker, such as ignorance or illiteracy or carelessness, whereas the second pair carries a connotation of desirable characteristics. These connotations are primarily a matter of social or cultural standing, and hence one may speak of cultural levels in the connotation of forms. Linguists distinguish primarily between forms that are *standard* (socially acceptable) and *nonstandard* (not socially acceptable).

There are native speakers who feel some substandard forms have greater clarity than standard forms do. To make the present-tense forms of the verb *to be* negative, one must use, in "correct" speech, three different forms: *I'm not, he isn't, we (you, they) aren't.* The "incorrect" *ain't,* however, offers one single form, exactly parallel to *can't, won't,* or *don't* and equally convenient. What is it, then, that makes some forms "incorrect" and others not? It is not a matter of authority or universal condemnation, but is simply a matter of acceptability in certain classes of our society. Approval of a form depends on whether hearers will react favorably or unfavorably toward a person they hear using it. "Correct" can only mean "socially acceptable," and apart from this the term has no meaning as applied to language.

The difference in social acceptability between *I ain't* and *I am not,* between *hern* and *hers,* and so forth, is a real fact. An indivifual's choice of language will be used by others as a purely arbitrary means of classifying him socially. All that is needed in the case of *I ain't,* for example, is to reword the traditional instructions and say that we avoid using such terms of speech, not because they are "bad" or "wrong" or "ungrammatical," but because they are socially unacceptable. Of course, as soon as people in any given group stop treating a term such as *he don't* as socially unacceptable, it automatically becomes "correct."[3]

Most American English vocabulary and usage falls in between the standard and the substandard, as well as between the formal and the informal. In combining these categories Robert A. Hall, Jr., produces four main types of usage:

Familiar standard:	He did it too soon.
Formal standard:	He did it prematurely.
Familiar substandard:	He done it too soon.
Formal substandard:	Between you and I.[4]

The last-mentioned category is the kind of speech one often hears from substandard speakers who try unsuccessfully to use formal standard language on occasions which they feel demand it.

Words are carried back and forth between nonstandard and standard English. Expressions that were at one time nonstandard may rise in the social scale and become standard, as has happened often in the history of English. The converse can also take place.

Perhaps one of the most significant aspects of standard English concerns language use in the home and in school. Many disadvantaged children speak either a dialect of English or an entirely different language. In either case, however well they communicate at home, their speech is often not that approved for classroom use. Although these children may daily hear standard English on television or radio, they often have little occasion to use the forms themselves and so come to school linguistically different. Nevertheless, they are expected to speak, read, and comprehend standard English.

It is not yet known why young children acquire the language forms they do and not others—why those who spend many hours in a day care center or in school hearing only standard English, or who in their homes listen to more television "talk" than adult conversation, still speak as their parents do.

The standardizing pressure of television, radio, and the movies will have an effect on speech patterns that are at variance with those dominant in a speech community. Such influences need reinforcement. However, the teacher's awareness of the social pressure exerted on those whose speech deviates from the forms of standard English may lead to an attempt to "correct" children's pronunciation and grammar. Except in courses specifically concerned with spoken English, teachers should be very slow to correct anyone's speech. Research shows that in the matter of grammatical form a child cannot go beyond the "rules" that he has worked out from his under-standing of language.

The notion of the need for grammatical "correctness" has been so strong as to form the basis for judgment of reading skill. If the printed page shows *She goes to school everyday and so does her brother* and the child reads *She go to school everday and so do her brother,* he is often held to be a poor reader, when in fact it is his regional or social dialect that is being judged, not his reading skill.

Though teachers are not in agreement about the value of some kinds of grammatical study, they do agree that all pupils should have the opportunity to acquire standard English and to understand the facts of usage. Knowledge of the structure of a language is also important for teachers themselves to have, because it guides the structure of thought in that language. An acquaintance with the structure of English, its history, development, and changing relation-ships, is part of the equipment for teaching.

Usage Changes Pronunciation and Meaning

Perhaps the subtlest of all grammatical processes is variations in accent, whether of stress or pitch. This is evident in such English doublets as *to refund* and *a refund, to extract* and *an extract, to come down* and *a come down,* and *to lack luster* and *lackluster,* in which the difference between the verb and the noun is entirely a matter of changing stress. Pitch accent may be as functional as stress and is perhaps more often so. Pitch variations, like stress and consonantal modifications, are phonetically essential to many languages, including English.

There can be little doubt that stress has frequently played a controlling influence in the formation of element groups or complex words out of certain sequences in the sentence. Such an English word as *withstand* is merely an old sequence *with stand,* or "against stand," in which the unstressed adverb was permanently drawn to the following verb and lost its independence as a significant element. But stress has done more than articulate or unify sequences that in their own right imply a syntactic relation. Stress is the most natural means at our disposal to emphasize linguistic contrast, to indicate the major element in a sequence.

Accent may serve as the unaided symbol of certain relations. Such a contrast as that of *go between* (one who goes between) and *to go between* may be of quite secondary origin in English, but there is every reason to believe that analogous distinctions have prevailed at all times in linguistic history.

Usage Changes Standards

Words like *in* and *of* appeared at the ends of sentences in Old English and have ever since. Anyone can object to them and try to get others to avoid them, but for those who use the preposition at the end of a sentence it is a matter of usage. Usage concerns the questions of right and wrong, or of appropriateness and inappropriateness in language.

A native speaker of a language has a most remarkable ability to subject his speech, as it is spoken, to continuous comparison with a standard. This standard is of his own compilation and is based on his observation of the speech of all those with whom he comes in contact. It is continually modified as his experience increases and as the speech around him changes. Pupils must be led to think objectively about their language, to be careful observants of the language of others, and to "try out" patterns of speech heard on radio and television in their conversations.

LANGUAGE AND WRITING

In conversation, the ordinary American is a confident, competent, expressive being. In writing he has a self-conscious horror of doing something wrong. A teacher who really wants to get good writing from pupils who know things, so that it is possible to learn what they know from their writing as easily as from their speech, must encourage written expression in the same style as oral expression. What matters is that one says what one has to say with no fumbling for the correct expression. The casual, brisk, colorful, amused, ironic, entertaining talk of American conversation is equally appropriate in print. Among other concerns in life, Americans prize individuality. Why then should everyone be expected to conform, especially since there is no general agreement on what to conform to, and one man's correctness is another's error?

Pupils must be led to see that there is more than one way to convey a message. The familiar pattern is only one method, neither inherently better nor worse than any other, and the structure used in any language can be judged only in the light of its place within its own coherent language system. The only feasible way to get such ideas across is by comparison of usages. The teacher must do this carefully and systematically, with thoughtful consideration of the materials used. And to be effective, the comparison must be undergirded with a comprehensive and defensible general view of language.[5]

To teach this comparative approach, classroom teachers must have a good grounding in linguistics. They do not, however, need to be acquainted with several languages, that is, beyond what is feasibly provided in a teacher's guide in a single lesson.

Writing should vary with the situation, the purpose, and the audience. There is no one single form of English that has general usefulness, nor would it be possible to agree on a set of standards for any reasonable number of specific varieties. Good written English does not fall into any finite number of definable types. Instead, there is multidimensional variation which produces an infinity of kinds of English, each with characteristics which may be useful in some situations.

There are significant differences between speaking and writing. One of these is that written material can be (and usually is) edited. An author goes back over his manuscript, changing a word here and a construction there. Or, in his writing he halts, sometimes for protracted periods, while he weighs alternatives, composing mentally several structures from which he can choose. Often he seeks (or has imposed) the advice and help of another. This editing process means that written English is a very much more precise production than spoken English is. More complex structures and more exact conformity to the conventions are expected. Good writing demands a greater competence with the patterns of the language and a greater sensitivity to certain aspects of style than does ordinary speech.

The tight structure of high-quality prose is found not only within sentences, but also in the sequencing of sentences within the passage. Indeed, there are probably more differences between good literary English and good colloquial English in the matter of transitions than in any features of the sentences considered separately. Readers and writers not thoroughly accustomed to this kind of language have real problems in this matter, and they need help with it. The scope of grammar must be extended to include the grammatical features of sentence relation. This brings in a number of topics hardly touched on in existing textbooks, and most of them are inadequately handled in the reference grammars as well.

RELUCTANCE TO ACCEPT CHANGE

The reluctance to accept change in language is shared by several groups: the public in general, educators, publishers. Change in anything is threatening. It is difficult to shake the terminology of traditional grammar. The grammar taught in the elementary school has long needed revision, but this has not been easy.

Linguists are impatient with the teacher's inertia to change. They feel it is as unrealistic to teach the "traditional" English grammar as it is to teach pre-Darwinian biology. Yet nearly all English teachers at all levels are doing so. Published materials dealing with language arts, on which grammar teaching is based, still have not broken with the school grammar of half a century ago.

Over the years research has failed to prove that traditional grammar has any effect on helping children speak or write better English. There is little research on the new grammar, but J. Stanley Sherwin notes that "so far, the experimental evidence supports the view that linguistics is about as effective as traditional grammar in improving writing."[6]

Unless emphasis is placed upon writing as a form of communication that is definitely directed to an actual, live reader, the importance of clarity, organization, and validity is not likely to become very apparent. Their importance becomes obvious the moment one seriously begins to *write about something for someone.* Then one does not just communicate; one communicates something to someone. The degree to which there is communication depends upon the degree to which the words represent the same thing for the receiver that they do for the sender.

The classroom is an ideal place for judging the clarity of both written and oral statements, because the sender and receiver are able to discuss the intent of the sender of the message and the understanding the receiver has of it. Improved clarity of statements and ideas through word choice, word order, and sentence order can be realized through practical applications.

A GRAMMATICAL REVOLUTION?

In 1954 W. Nelson Francis wrote the widely publicized and often-quoted "Revolution in Grammar."[7] Today one wonders whatever happened to the grammatical revolution. Much has been written about linguistics, semantics, dialects. The theory has been expounded at length, but the revolution has not been evident in practice. John F. Savage believes that the new grammar has remained outside many classroom doors because of a combination of reasons, which generally include:

1. A lack of training in linguistics and knowledge of the new grammar.
2. A lack of materials that will allow teachers to do a good job in teaching the new grammar.
3. A general reluctance to change the traditional grammar that has become a sacred cow in the curriculum.[8]

H. A. Gleason, Jr. feels that the English teaching profession has been preparing for revolutionary changes for two generations. There will be changes in certain features of English grammar and perhaps more in the bases of style. English faces a revolution, not only in its representation in the school curriculum but in its organization for research. The principle that language has structure and system is fundamental, but grammar is the study of the structure and system of language in one of its more significant aspects. An integrated English curriculum which is to deal adequately with the proper concerns must make grammar an important element. To serve in a new curriculum, grammar must be rehabilitated, given a new content and a new image.[9]

To be able to teach the new grammar the teacher must have some prior training that is more than just memorization of definitions and rules. Some teachers have not been trained in grammar or language study at all, due to the common belief that anyone who can speak English can teach it. The teacher must have both a technical vocabulary adequate to the task and some skill in approaching language analytically.

Many teachers are unfamiliar with the content of the new grammar. Some theories have been made needlessly complicated, difficult to learn, and difficult to teach. As teachers begin to realize that language itself is an intricate phenomenon, they will find that the linguistic-based language and grammar approach makes sense in terms of accuracy in describing our language.

Lack of adequate classroom materials has been a drawback to teaching the new terminology and the broader aspects of language. This is especially true in the elementary grades. Perhaps the area that has received the most consideration is the history of language. Segments of information on this topic have been included in some series of spellers and language arts textbooks, and material dealing with word histories is at hand in any good dictionary. In any case, unless materials are used properly, they can only perpetuate the dogmatism of the early grammarians.

The grammatical revolution requires extensive retraining in attitudes toward language. Teachers must broaden their horizons; rather than focusing on a few errors, they must generalize and compare and contrast constructions. This will require penetrating more deeply into the traditional subject matter of the structure of sentences. Many of the patterns in the traditional approach have been those with which the pupil has very little trouble. Study of the history of our language and of how certain grammatical structures have been established should prepare teachers to be more helpful with the more unusual patterns.

SUGGESTIONS AND ACTIVITIES FOR THE COLLEGE STUDENT AND THE CLASSROOM TEACHER

1. There are some educators who feel fully justified to conclude that "linguistics is just like the functional grammar idea of the twenties." Do you agree? Can you defend linguistics as a science?
2. The vogue of "functional grammar" in the 1920s and 1930s as a replacement for "formal grammar" was an achievement of educational theorists rather than of English teachers themselves. It meant the teaching of grammar only where and when it was needed. Can you support the philosophy of functional grammar from research?

3. Linguistic scientists have stated that "there are many different kinds of grammar." The general public and some teachers cling to the traditional grammar concept. Can you support those who feel there can be only one grammar—the one in the textbook they used in elementary school? If not, what is your position on the grammar controversy?

4. Form two groups or committees. Let one group research and support one or more of the current grammars and the other support the concept of usage. Present the material as a debate, panel, or interview.

5. Consult several sources for definitions of language, grammar, usage, semantics, and linguistics. Use such sources as dictionaries, encyclopedias, traditional grammars, books by linguists and linguistic scientists. In small groups discuss your interpretations of the meanings found. Discussion areas might be, "When I hear the word 'grammar' my interpretation of the way the word is used is _____." "When I use the word 'semantics,' I want the listener to infer that I mean _____."

6. From time to time there have been statements in the press that if there is to be a world languge, that language should be and probably will be English. The only serious limitation of English arises from its spelling. It is especially difficult for one who does not learn English as a native tongue. Would you advocate revising our spelling to fit our pronunciation or revising our pronunciation to fit our spelling? How can you promote English as a world language?

7. Do you agree that a great deal of hard work by a great many people is necessary to do anything effective with linguistics in the schools? As one teacher in a school system, what can be your role in promoting a study of our language?

8. In general those groups of children in the United States who are in the lowest income brackets and who achieve the least in school are also victims of the color bar. As a teacher, what can you do to raise the standard of teaching-learning for the Mexican-American, the black, or the Indian child in your school?

9. A first requisite for the teacher of communication arts is an awareness of his own limited knowledge and a determination to expand his acquaintance with the structure of our language. If you agree with this statement, how can you go about extending

your information? If you don't agree with this statement, what requisite should take precedence over this statement?

10. In a recent article Ladislas Orszagh states that a dictionary is needed to describe the associative possibilities of words and their usage in the English language for those whose native language is not English.[10] Such a dictionary would give commonly used combinations of words from a semantic point of view and would focus on examples of general usage rather than on those from literature. How could a speaker of another language apply the material in a dictionary focusing on combinations of words frequently used by Americans? Would such a dictionary be feasible?

NOTES

1. Joseph H. Friend, *An Introduction to English Linguistics* (Cleveland: The World Book Publishing Co. 1967), p. 21.

2. Ibid., pp. 105-06.

3. Robert A. Hall, Jr., *Linguistics and Your Language* (Garden City, New York: Doubleday & Co., 1950), p. 13.

4. Ibid., p. 130.

5. H. A. Gleason, Jr., *Linguistics and English Grammar* (New York: Holt, Rinehart & Winston, Inc., 1965), p. 486.

6. J. Stanley Sherwin, *Four Problems in Teaching English: A Critique of Research* (Scranton, Pa: International Textbook Co., 1969), p. 168.

7. W. Nelson Francis, "Revolution in Grammar," *Quarterly Journal of Speech,* 40 (1954): 299-312.

8. John F. Savage, "Whatever Happened to the Grammatical Revolution?" *Elementary English,* 49 (1972): 599.

9. H. A. Gleason, Jr., *Linguistics and English Grammar,* p. 472.

10. Ladislas Orszagh, "Wanted: Better English Dictionaries," *English Language Teaching* 23 (1968), pp. 216-22.

Bibliography

Aiken, Janet Rankin. *A New Plan of English Grammar.* New York: Henry Holt & Co., 1933.

Alexander, Hubert G. *Meaning in Language.* Glenview, Ill.: Scott, Foresman & Co., 1969.

Anisfeld, Moshe, and Tucker, G. Richard. "English Pluralization Rules of Six-Year-Old Children." *Child Development* 38(1967): 1201–17.

Barnett, Lincoln. *The Treasure of Our Tongue.* New York: Alfred A. Knopf, 1964.

Baugh, Albert C. *A History of the English Language,* 2d ed. New York: Appleton-Century-Crofts, 1957.

Bellugi, Ursula, and Brown, Roger W., eds. *The Acquisition of Language.* Monograph from Cognitive Development in Children—Society for Research in Child Development. Chicago: University of Chicago Press, 1972.

Bereiter, Carl, and Engelmann, Siegfried. *Teaching Disadvantaged Children in the Preschool.* Englewood Cliffs, N.J.: Prentice-Hall, 1966.

Berko, J. "The Child's Learning of English Morphology." *Word,* 14 (1958): 150–77.

Berlo, David K. *The Process of Communication: An Introduction to Theory and Practice.* New York: Holt, Rinehart & Winston, 1960.

Bloomfield, Leonard. *Language.* New York: Henry Holt & Co., 1933.

Boyd, Gertrude A. *Poetry in the Elementary School.* Columbus, Ohio: Charles E. Merrill Publishing Co., 1973.

————. *Teaching Communication Skills in the Elementary School.* New York: Van Nostrand Reinhold Co., 1970.

Brackbill, Yvonne, ed. *Infancy and Early Childhood.* New York: Free Press, 1967.

Braine, M. D. S. "The Ontogeny of the English Phrase Structure: The First Phrase." *Language,* 39(1963): 1–13.

Brown, Marshall L. *Language: The Origins of English.* Columbus, Ohio: Charles E. Merrill Publishing Co., 1971.

Brown, Roger, and Bellugi, Ursula. "Three Processes in the Child's Acquisition of Syntax." *Harvard Educational Review,* 34(1964): 133–51.

Brown, Roger W., and Fraser, Colin. "The Acquisition of Syntax." *Child Development Monographs,* 39(1964): 43–79.

Brown, Roger W.; Cazden, Courtney B.; and Bellugi, Ursula. "The Child's Grammar from 1 to 111." In *Minnesota Symposium on Child Psychology,* 5 vols. Minneapolis: University of Minnesota Press, 1968–1971.

Bryant, Margaret M. *Modern English and Its Heritage,* 2d ed. New York: Macmillan Co., 1962.

Bryant, Margaret, and Aiken, Janet. *Psychology of English.* New York: Columbia University Press, 1940.

Carlson, Putricia, and Anisfeld, Moshe. "Some Observations on the Linguistic Competence of a Two-Year-Old Child." *Child Development,* 40(1969): 569–75.

Cazden, Courtney B. "The Acquisition of Noun and Verb Inflections." Unpublished paper, Harvard University, 1967.

————. "Children's Questions: Their Forms, Functions, and Roles in Education." *Young Children,* 25 (1970): 202–20.

————. "Environmental Assistance to the Child's Acquisition of Grammar." Ph.D. dissertation, Harvard University, 1965.

Chomsky, Noam. *Aspects of the Theory of Syntax.* Cambridge, Mass.: M.I.T. Press, 1969.

————. "Comments for Project Literacy Meeting." *Project Literacy Reports,* September 1964, pp. 1–8.

————. *Syntactic Structures.* The Hugue: Mouton, 1957.

Dean, Leonard F., and Wilson, Kenneth G. *Essays on Language and Usage,* 2d ed. New York: Oxford University Press, 1963.

Deutsch, Martin. "The Role of Social Class in Language Development and Cognition." *American Journal of Orthopsychiatry,* 25(1965): 78–88.

Dykema, Karl. "Where Our Grammar Came From." *College English,* 22(1961): 455–65.

Emig, Janet A., ed. *Language and Learning.* New York: Harcourt, Brace & World, 1966.

Emig, Janet A.; Fleming, James T.; and Popp, Helen M. *Language and Learning.* New York: Harcourt, Brace & World, 1964.

Encroyd, D. H. "Negro Children and Language Arts." *Reading Teacher,* 21(1968): 624–29.

Ervin, S. M., and Foster, George. "The Development of Meaning in Children's Descriptive Terms." *Journal of Abnormal and Social Psychology,* 61(1960): 271–75.

Ervin, Susan M., and Miller, W. R. "Language Development." In *Child Psychology,* 62d Yearbook of the National Society for the Study of Education, edited by H. W. Stevenson. Chicago: University of Chicago Press, 1963.

Fagan, William T. "Transformations and Comprehension." *The Reading Teacher,* 25(1971): 169–72.

Francis, Hazel. "Structure in the Speech of a 2½-Year-Old." *British Journal of Educational Psychology,* 39(1969): 291–302.

Francis, W. Nelson. "Revolution in Grammar." *Quarterly Journal of Speech,* 40 (1954): 221–28.

Friend, Joseph H. *An Introduction to English Linguistics.* Cleveland: World Book Publishing Co., 1967.

Fries, Charles Carpenter. *The Structure of English.* New York: Harcourt, Brace & World, 1952.

Gardiner, Alan H. "The Definition of the Word and the Sentence." *British Journal of Psychiatry,* 12(1922).

Gardiner, Allan H. *Theory of Speech and Language,* 2d ed. Oxford: Clarendon Press, 1951.

Gleason, H. A., Jr. *Linguistics and English Grammar.* New York: Holt, Rinehart & Winston, 1965.

———. "What Grammar?" *Harvard Educational Review,* 34 (1964): 216–32.

Graves, Michael F., and Koziol, Stephen. "Noun Plural Development in Primary Grade Children." *Child Development,* 42(1971): 1165–73.

Greenough, J. B., and Kittredge, George Lyman. *Words and Their Ways in English Speech.* New York: Macmillan Co., 1961.

Hall, Robert A., Jr. *Linguistics and Your Language,* rev. ed. Garden City, N.Y.: Doubleday & Co., 1950.

Haupt, Dorothy. "Teacher-Child Interaction: A Study of the Relationships between Child-Initiated Questions and Nursery School Teacher Behaviors." Ph.D. dissertation, Wayne State University, Detroit, 1966.

Hayakawa, S. I. *Language in Thought and Action,* 3rd ed. New York: Harcourt Brace Jovanovich, 1972.

Herriot, Peter. "The Comprehension of Syntax." *Child Development,* 39(1968): 273–82.

Hess, R. D., and Shipman, V. C. "Early Experience and the Socialization of Cognitive Modes in Children." *Child Development,* 36(1966): 869–86.

Hill, Archibald A. *Introduction to Linguistic Structures.* New York: Harcourt, Brace & World, 1958.

Hill, John P., ed. *Minnesota Symposium on Child Psychology,* 5 vols. Minneapolis: University of Minnesota Press, 1968–1971.

Hook, J. N., Crowell, Michael G. *Modern English Grammar for Teachers.* New York: Ronald Press Co., 1970.

Houston, Susan H. "A Reexamination of Some Assumptions about the Language of the Disadvantaged Child." *Child Development,* 41(1970): 947–63.

———. "A Sociolinguistic Consideration of the Black English of Children in Northern Florida." *Language,* 45(1969): 599–607.

Isaacs, N. Appendix on Children's "Why" Questions. In *Intellectual Growth in Young Children,* by Susan Isaacs. New York: Shocken Books, 1966.

Jespersen, Otto. *Essentials of English Grammar* (1933). Reprinted, Tuscaloosa, Ala.: University of Alabama Press, 1964.

———. *Growth and Structure of the English Language,* 9th ed. New York: Free Press, 1968.

———. *Language: Its Nature, Development, and Origin.* New York: W. W. Norton & Co., 1964.

John, V. P. "The Intellectual Development of Slum Children: Some Preliminary Findings." *American Journal of Orthopsychiatry,* 33(1963): 813–22.

Joos, Martin. "Language and the School Child." In *Language and Learning,* edited by Janet A. Emig. New York: Harcourt, Brace & World, 1966, pp. 102–11.

Kerr, Elizabeth M., and Aderman, Ralph M., eds. *Aspects of American English,* 2d ed. New York: Harcourt Brace Jovanovich, 1971.

Kirby, Thomas A., and Woolf, Henry Bosley, eds. *Philologics: The Malone Anniversary Studies.* Baltimore: Johns Hopkins University Press, 1949.

Korzybski, Alfred. *Science and Sanity: An Introduction to Non-Aristotelian Systems and General Semantics,* 4th ed. Lakeville, Conn.: International Non-Aristotelian Library Publishing Co., 1958.

Langacker, R. W. *Language and Its Structure.* New York: Harcourt Brace & World, 1968.

Lavatelli, Celia Stendler. "An Approach to Language Learning." *Young Children,* 24(1969): 368–76.

Lee, Laura L. "The Relevance of General Semantics to the Development of Sentence Structure in Children's Language." In *Communication: General Semantics Perspectives,* edited by Lee Thayer. New York: Spartan Books, 1970.

Lenneberg, E. H. "The Capacity for Language Acquisition." In *The Structure of Language,* edited by Jerry Foder and J. J. Katz. Englewood Cliffs, N.J.: Prentice-Hall, 1964.

Lewis, Morris M. *Language, Thought and Personality.* New York: Basic Books, 1964.

Lowth, Robert. *A Short Introduction to English Grammar.* Menston, England: The Scholar Press, 1775. Originally published 1762.

Marckwardt, Albert H. *American English.* New York: Oxford University Press, 1958.

Mencken, H. L. *The American Language,* 4th ed. 3 vols. New York: Alfred A. Knopf, 1948.

———. *The American Language.* Supplement One. New York: Alfred A. Knopf, 1945.

———. "The Birth of New Verbs." In *Philologica: The Malone Anniversary Studies,* edited by Thomas A. Kirby and Henry Bosley Woolf. Baltimore: Johns Hopkins University Press, 1949.

Menninger, Karl, et al. *The Vital Balance: The Life Process in Mental Health and Illness.* New York: Viking Press, 1967.

Menyuk, Paula. "Syntactic Rules Used by Children from Preschool through First Grade." *Child Development,* 35(1964): 533–46.

Menyuk, Paula, and Bernholtz, N. *Prosodic Features and Children's Language Production.* Quarterly Progress Report No. 93, M.I.T. Research Laboratory on Electronics, April 1969.

Milgram, Norman A.; Shore, Milton F.; and Malasky, Charlotte. "Linguistic and Thematic Variables in Recall of a Story by Disadvantaged Children." *Child Development,* 42(19716: 637–40.

Miller, William. "New Sentence Tactics through Predication." *College Composition and Communication,* 22(1971): 365–76.

Miller, W. R., and Ervin, S. M. "The Development of Grammar in Child Language." *Child Development Monographs,* 39(1964): 9–34.

Myers, L. M., and Montague, Gene. *Guide to American English,* 5th ed. Englewood Cliffs, N.J.: Prentice-Hall, 1.72.

Natalicio, Diana S., and Natalicio, Luiz F. S. "A Comparative Study of English Pluralization by Native and Non-Native English Speakers." *Child Development,* 42(1971): 1302–6.

Ogden, Charles K., and Richards, Ivor A. *The Meaning of Meaning.* New York: Harcourt, Brace & Co., 1952.

Pei, Mario. *The Story of English.* Greenwich, Conn.: Fawcett Publications, 1952.

Postman, Neil, and Weingartner, Charles. *Linguistics: A Revolution in Teaching.* New York: Dell Publishing Co., 1966.

Priestley, Joseph. *The Rudiments of English Grammar,* 2d ed. London: R. Griffiths, 1771.

Pyles, Thomas. *Words and Ways of American English.* New York: Random House, 1963.

Rebelsky, Freda G.; Starr, Raymond H., Jr.; and Luria, Zella. "Language Development—The First Four Years." In *Infancy and Early Childhood,* edited by Yvonne Brackbill. New York: Free Press, 1967.

Roberts, Paul M. *Understanding English.* New York: Harper & Bros., 1958.

Robertson, Stuart, and Cassidy, F. G. *The Development of Modern English,* 2d. ed. Englewood Cliffs, N.J.: Prentice-Hall, 1954.

Robins, Robert H. *Ancient and Medieval Grammatical Theory in Europe.* Port Washington, N.Y.: Kennikat Press Corp., 1971. Originally published 1951.

Rommetveit, Ragnar. *Words, Meanings, and Messages.* New York: Academic Press, 1968.

Rycenga, John A., and Schwartz, Joseph, eds. *Perspectives on Language: An Anthology.* New York: Ronald Press, 1963.

Sapir, Edward. *Language: An Introduction to the Study of Speech.* New York: Harcourt, Brace & World, 1921.

Savage, John F. "Whatever Happened to the Grammatical Revolution?" *Elementary English,* 49(April 1972): 599–663.

Schlauch, Margaret. *The Gift of Language.* New York: Dover Publications, 1955.

Sherwin, J. Stanley. *Four Problems in Teaching English: A Critique of Research.* Scranton, Pa.: International Textbook Co., 1969.

Templin, Mildred C. *Certain Language Skills in Children.* Child Welfare Monograph Series No. 26. Minneapolis: University of Minnesota Press, 1957.

Thayer, Lee, ed. *Communication: General Semantics Perspectives.* New York: Spartan Books, 1970.

Turner, Elizabeth Ann, and Rommetveit, Ragnar. "The Acquisition of Sentence Voice and Reversibility." *Child Development,* 38(1967): 649–60.

Vygotsky, Lev S. *Thought and Language.* New York: John Wiley & Sons, 1963.

Walcott, F. G.; Thorpe, C. D.; and Savage, S. P. *Growth in Thought and Expression.* Chicago: Benjamin H. Sanborn & Co., 1940.

Weingartner, Charles. "Semantics: What and Why." *English Journal,* 58(1969): 1214–19.

Werner, Heinz, and Kaplan, Bernard. *Symbol Formation.* New York: John Wiley & Sons, 1963.

INDEX

(Italicized page numbers refer to citation at the end of the chapters.)

THE BOOK MANUFACTURE

Linguistics in the Elementary School was typeset at Progressive Typographers, Inc., and printed and bound at the George Banta Company, Inc., Menasha, Wisconsin. Cover design was by Charles Kling & Associates. The type is Times Roman with Helvetica display.

LANGUAGE ARTS SERIES

Paul C. Burns, Editor
University of Tennessee

DIAGNOSTIC TEACHING OF THE LANGUAGE ARTS

Paul C. Burns

**LANGUAGE ARTS FOR THE EXCEPTIONAL:
THE GIFTED AND THE LINGUISTICALLY DIFFERENT**

Lester N. Knight

CREATIVE DRAMA IN THE ELEMENTARY SCHOOL

Barbara M. McIntyre

LINGUISTICS IN THE ELEMENTARY SCHOOL

Gertrude A. Boyd

**LANGUAGE EXPERIENCES FOR NURSERY
AND KINDERGARTEN YEARS**

Gertrude B. Corcoran

LINGUISTICS IN THE ELEMENTARY SCHOOL